Seeking My Legacy

Dr. Stephanie West, EdD

ISBN 979-8-89112-335-9 (Paperback)
ISBN 979-8-89112-336-6 (Digital)

Covenant Books
11661 Hwy 707
Murrells Inlet, SC 29576
www.covenantbooks.com

Contents

What Is Legacy? v

Part 1: Husband, Children, Pets—Oh My!
Chapter 1:   Marriage to My Best Friend 3
Chapter 2:   Children, Oh My! 19
Chapter 3:   My Prodigal Son 33
Chapter 4:   Grown Children and Grandchildren 43

Part 2: Following Your Passions—the Place beyond Dreams
Chapter 5:   Becoming a Teacher 55
Chapter 6:   Changing the World One Student at a Time 65

Part 3: Staying the Course, No Matter What
Chapter 7:   Trials, Anxiety, Depression......................................87
Chapter 8:   Serving Those around Me 106
Chapter 9:   My Testimony of Christ 123

What Is Your Legacy?...129

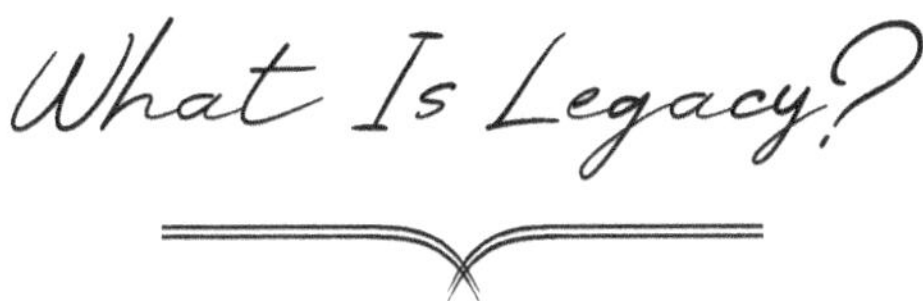

The goal isn't to live forever, the goal is
to create something that will.
—Chuck Palahniuk

Amidst the somber atmosphere of the funeral home chapel, she stood beside her husband of forty-six years, tears streaming down her face, grappling with the overwhelming reality of his absence. Her beloved husband had succumbed to the devastating COVID-19 virus just a week ago. As she gazed at their legacy, ten children with their partners and thirty grandchildren, a profound sense of loss engulfed her. Seeking solace one last time, she placed her head on her childhood sweetheart's chest, unable to suppress her sorrow. The room fell silent as she wept, trying to bid farewell to the boy who became a man she had cherished throughout their lives together. The bond they formed at the tender age of fourteen remained unbreakable even in death. As she contemplated a future without him, she faced the daunting task of moving forward, uncertain of how to navigate life without her constant companion by her side.

As I stood amidst the heart-wrenching scene, my emotions torn, I turned to my husband, her brother, and found myself at a loss for words to comfort either of them. Tears streamed down my face as I wrapped my arms around him, seeking to offer whatever solace I could, as I have done for the past thirty-four years. The sight before us was unbearable, the tragedy so unexpected. We found ourselves grappling with the overwhelming reality of the moment, uncertain of how we arrived here and where to go from this point onward. Helplessly, we bore witness to the profound pain that surrounded us, the sight of hearts breaking and the sound of both young and grown children openly weeping. In this moment of sorrow, we stood united, trying to hold each other together amidst the grief and loss.

In the span of just four short months earlier, I remember myself standing next to my mother, this time to bid farewell to my father, whom she had been married to for an incredible fifty-eight years. Their love story began when my mom was merely nineteen and my dad, twenty-three.

As we gathered in the funeral home chapel, surrounded by our extended family of nine grown children and their spouses, even a couple of ex-spouses whom my dad cherished, I couldn't help but notice the thirty grandchildren and twelve great-grandchildren who were silently grieving. During our collective sorrow, my mom, the steadfast rock of our family, remained composed and dignified, gracefully greeting lifelong friends and family and offering comfort to my siblings, nieces, and nephews. The weight of our losses felt immeasurable, and yet in these moments of grief, we found strength in one another and in the legacy of love that our parents had built throughout their extraordinary journey together.

I remember clearly on that day when the bishop entered the room, signaling that it was time for the family prayer, I sought comfort in my husband's presence. The passing of my father was not unexpected; he had been battling heart issues for several years. He was fortunate to pass away peacefully in his sleep, at ease in the comfort of his home and favorite chair. Yet even with the knowledge that his suffering had come to an end, the moment arrived to close the lid of the casket, a poignant reminder of the finality of his departure.

Each of my siblings took their turn saying their farewells, whether through whispered words, tears, or a simple touch of his hand for one last time. My mother, my pillar of strength, also bid her final goodbye. As my older brother led the prayer, the casket was gently closed, signifying the conclusion of my father's earthly journey. Reflecting on the words of Paul, who urged us to "finish our course with joy and the ministry we have received from the Lord Jesus" (Acts 20:24), I couldn't help but wonder if we were truly living up to this counsel in our own lives.

Funerals are truly unique events, encompassing a myriad of emotions and experiences. During my dad's funeral, our family came together, reuniting all nine children after more than eight years. It was a time of tears, laughter, and heartfelt conversations. We shared genuine moments with one another, reminiscing about cherished memories and telling stories that reflected the essence of my dad's life.

As we listened to spiritual talks centered around the plan of salvation, we were reminded of the profound impact his life had on all of us. Each sibling took their turn in sharing a personal story or a cherished memory of our dad, painting a beautiful tapestry of his legacy. In those moments, we recognized the depth of his influence on our lives and the lasting impression he left on each one of us. Funerals serve as poignant reminders of the legacy our loved ones leave behind, and my dad's funeral was a poignant testament to the love, joy, and wisdom he imparted upon us all.

But what is a legacy? Do we understand the meaning of that word? A legacy, as defined by *Merriam-Webster*, is something transmitted from the past, an inheritance from our ancestors or predecessors. I find this definition intriguing as it conveys the idea of passing something meaningful to future generations. To transmit implies that we are imparting valuable knowledge, experiences, and virtues to our posterity for their betterment. It involves sharing the lessons we have learned, both the successes and the setbacks, as a source of guidance and inspiration. Every day, I find myself continuously learning, not just about myself but also about those around me and how I can become a better person, a more devout Christian, and a more compassionate servant of my faith. Embracing this concept of legacy means understanding the profound impact we can have on the lives of those who come after us, leaving behind a positive imprint that stretches beyond our own time on this earth.

Reflecting on life experiences, funeral talks, and life sketches of those who have passed away leaves me with introspective questions about my own legacy. What am I leaving behind for my children and those around me? Have I imparted enough wisdom and guidance for them to confidently stand on their own? Do people remember me as a good person, someone who stood for something and served others? Pres. Gordon B. Hinckley's words, "Stand for Something," resonate with me, urging me to examine whether I have lived a life of strong convictions and unwavering testimony. I hope my loved ones, from children to grandchildren and great-grandchildren, will know the depth of my love for Christ, our Heavenly Father, and for them. I aspire for them to remember me as someone who encouraged and supported others in finding and pursuing their passions and dreams. Ultimately, I seek reassurance that my children are finding fulfillment in their pursuits and that my legacy leaves a positive impact on their lives and the lives of those around me.

Within the pages of this book, you will find fragments of my life and personal journey. I do not claim expertise in the subject of leaving behind a legacy, but my hope is that by sharing my story, you will discover inspiration to craft your own narrative and legacy. Throughout these chapters, I recount the trials and tribulations I faced, from navigating marriage and parenthood to balancing a career as a working mother and educator. Above all, this book sheds light on my identity as a daughter of God, delving into my Christian beliefs with a focus on the Church of Jesus Christ of Latter-day Saints. While I understand that this perspective may not resonate with everyone, I share my experiences and the lessons I have learned in the hopes that they may connect with you in your own life's struggles. I openly discuss my battles with deep depression and severe anxiety, seeking to provide solace and support to those facing similar challenges. My intention is to offer guidance and encouragement to help you find your own unique legacy, whether it involves building upon existing foundations or making transformative changes in your life. My desire is for you to leave a legacy for your posterity that fills you with pride and purpose.

Creating a meaningful and lasting legacy is not a singular event but rather a continuous narrative that unfolds throughout our lives. It is a unique and personal story, shaped by our experiences, choices, and values. It is my story, and it is your story. Together, let us embark on this journey of discovering and nurturing our legacies. Let us embrace the lessons from the past, live purposefully in the present, and envision the impact we want to leave on future generations. By joining hands and hearts, we can support and inspire one another as we strive to build a legacy that reflects the essence of who we are and the values we hold dear.

> We are bidden to "put on Christ," to become like God.
> That is, whether we like it or not, God intends to give
> us what we need, not what we now think we want.
> —C. S. Lewis

Part 1

Husband, Children, Pets—Oh My!

The family is ordained of God.
—The family proclamation

In life, just like the Cowardly Lion in *The Wizard of Oz*, we often encounter moments of fear and uncertainty. Whether it's stepping into a new marriage or embracing the responsibility of raising children, these pivotal moments can be intimidating. However, with the support and encouragement of our loved ones, we find the strength to face our fears and move forward.

Each member of our family plays a significant role in shaping not only our individual legacies but also the legacy of our entire family. Like the phrase "Lions, tigers, bears—oh my," we face challenges, but with love and unity, we can navigate through the trials and create a meaningful and lasting family legacy. Husband, children, pets—oh my!

Chapter 1

Marriage to My Best Friend

"Marriage is ordained of God" for His children.
—Doctrine and Covenants 49:15

Whatsoever God doeth, it shall be forever.
—Ecclesiastes 3:14

Some of my family's most cherished and amusing anecdotes center around the captivating tale of my husband and my courtship. It followed the typical Mormon traditions as I was merely nineteen years old, and he was twenty-one when we first crossed paths at a vibrant young adult dance. Our romance unfolded rapidly as we dated for a mere six weeks before realizing we were destined for each other and decided to take the plunge into engagement. Six months later, amidst the sacred walls of the temple, we exchanged our vows and committed ourselves to a lifelong journey together.

Though it may seem like an effortless and straightforward narrative, the reality was quite different. While I have no doubt that I married the perfect person for me, it wasn't immediately evident to my family, particularly my dad, who took some time to come around and see the true bond and love we shared. Our journey together has been a testament to the strength of our love and the power of time to dissolve any initial reservations, proving that true love always finds its way.

On that warm summer night, the Saturday preceding Labor Day in 1986, my heart skipped a beat as I found myself standing in the cultural hall of the stake center. Amidst the lively atmosphere, my attention was drawn to a handsome boy seated on the stage, whose gaze was fixed on me. With each playful point and whispered exchange to his friend, a smile that could melt hearts adorned his face, captivating me entirely.

Uncertain of what he was conveying or why I had become the subject of his attention, I was unable to tear my gaze away from him. His presence was magnetic, and that disarming smile of his rendered me powerless. He was undeniably attractive, boasting muscular arms that hinted at his gymnastic past and his stint as a yell leader in high school. Oh, those dimples—despite knowing I shouldn't use such a word to describe my future husband—they were simply too cute and irresistible to ignore. With his glasses and suspenders, he embraced the fashion of the '80s with charming flair.

And then, as the dance drew to a close, to the beats of "Footloose," he mustered the courage to ask me for a dance. His name was Scott, and we shared just one dance that night, parting ways with a lingering sense of curiosity and excitement. Little did I know that this serendipitous encounter would be the beginning of a remarkable journey filled with love and cherished memories.

The following week, destiny played its hand once again as I found myself at the same place, same time, and there he was—my captivating guy, standing on the stage as if it were his designated spot at these dances. This time, I was accompanied by my older brother and his friend, who happened to be my brother's former missionary companion, hoping to set us up. Yet my heart yearned for the charming boy with the infectious smile and strong arms, and I couldn't fathom being interested in anyone else. I held on to the hope that something deeper might blossom between us.

Uncertain of my dating situation, Scott observed patiently, waiting for an opportunity to approach me when I was alone. Finally, he mustered the courage to ask me to dance, and from that moment on, he kept me on the dance floor for the remainder of the night. We conversed, danced, and shared smiles that spoke volumes. There was an inexplicable connection between us, a familiarity that made it feel as though we had known each other forever.

Conversing with him was effortless, and dancing together was an absolute delight. The comfort and ease in his presence were like nothing I had experienced before. It was as if we were kindred spirits, destined to meet at that precise moment in time. But little did I know, this enchanting encounter was only the beginning of a love story that would touch the depths of our souls and transcend the bounds of time.

A few weeks before, I had made the difficult decision to let go of my missionary. At nineteen, I was focused on my studies, trying to pave my own path, and marriage was not part of the immediate plan. Scott's presence both exhilarated and frightened me; he seemed to disrupt my carefully laid-out plans. There were so many things I wanted to experience, places to explore, and people to meet. Yet whenever I was with Scott, I felt an inexplicable sense of completeness and ease. Conversations with him flowed effortlessly, and he genuinely listened to my aspirations of becoming a teacher and supported my dreams wholeheartedly, just as I did with his. Although he had already served as a missionary and was only twenty-one, we were both remarkably young, with an entire lifetime ahead of us to consider settling down. The question lingered: was I ready for such a commitment?

However, as time went on, Scott's unwavering presence in my life gradually reshaped my plans, making room for him to be an integral part of not just my present but also my future, extending into the eternities. He had a way of changing my perspective and inspiring a newfound readiness to embrace the beautiful journey of life together, and ultimately, he became an irreplaceable piece of my heart's puzzle.

Scott and I found ourselves falling head over heels in love with each other at an astonishing speed, our hearts entwined in a passionate whirlwind. The connection between us was so undeniable and profound that we both knew without a doubt that we had found our soulmate in each other. Little did we realize that my perceptive father-in-law had already sensed the depth of our love and beat my husband to the punch by expressing his heartfelt blessing for our potential union. His kind words filled me with warmth and joy, assuring me that if our love stood the test of time, I had his whole-hearted approval to marry his son.

This touching gesture, unbeknownst to Scott, happened to coincide with the very day he had planned to propose, and he worried it might have ruined his intentions. However, I was utterly delighted and overwhelmed by my father-in-law's support, and it didn't diminish the significance of Scott's heartfelt proposal that came later that evening, delivered in his own unique way. Knowing that I had my future father-in-law's blessing made the moment all the more special. As the years passed, my bond with my father-in-law deepened, evolving into a cherished and unbreakable relationship that continues to hold a special place in my heart to this very day.

The day after Scott's official proposal, we mustered the courage to share the exciting news with my family. Gathering in the living room, with all nine of my siblings miraculously present, tension filled the air. My dad occupied his chair on the far wall, while my mom sat on the end of the couch nearest to us. As Scott and I sat down, I found myself rendered speechless, unable to articulate the news. Scott, sensing the weight of the moment, took charge and bravely announced our decision to get married.

Instantly, all eyes turned to my dad, and the room fell into an eerie silence. It was the kind of silence that hung heavily, thick with uncertainty. Fear engulfed me as I anxiously awaited my father's response, desperately seeking his approval. My dad, my hero, had the power to make or break my dreams. Minutes dragged on, or so it felt, with my dad's gaze unwavering and Scott holding his ground.

Just when I thought the silence would never end, my mom broke it by asking a simple question about our wedding plans. Relieved that my mom had spoken up, Scott and I made our exit from the house, allowing my parents the space they needed to process the news. Years later, we learned that the announcement had deeply upset them, prompting them to seek solace and understanding by retreating on a camping trip, leaving just the two of them to grapple with their emotions. As time would reveal, their initial reservations eventually transformed into unwavering love and support for our marriage, allowing us to embark on this journey together, knowing we had the blessings of those we cherished most.

Fast-forward six months to a beautiful March day in 1987, and there I was, sitting outside the Mesa, Arizona, temple, eagerly awaiting Scott's arrival so we could enter the temple together. With my parents by my side, I held my wedding dress and temple clothes in my arms, brimming with excitement. However, time seemed to stretch on endlessly as we waited, and Scott was nowhere to be seen. My heart sank when I learned he had forgotten his temple recommend and had to dash back home, which was fortunately just a short distance away from the temple. He ended up being only about five minutes late, but each passing moment felt like an eternity.

My father, ever protective, couldn't bear the thought of Scott not showing up and promptly grabbed my wedding dress, saying we should go home. My mother, however, urged him to be patient. I was on the verge of tears, fervently praying for Scott's timely arrival. And then, like a beacon of hope, I spotted Scott running down the sidewalk, bringing immense relief to my anxious heart. In that moment, all worries faded away, and I knew that everything was going to be just fine.

The day of our wedding turned out to be nothing short of perfection. The majestic temple stood resplendent under the radiant sun, setting the stage for a truly magical occasion. Our families gathered around us, creating an atmosphere of love and togetherness. Throughout the day, we witnessed the rekindling of old connections within the family, fostering a sense of unity and joy. Smiles adorned every face and laughter echoed in the air as an abundance of love overflowed from every heart present. In those blissful moments, I was certain beyond a shadow of a doubt that I had made the most profound and right decision of my life in marrying this remarkable man, whose heart and soul were now eternally intertwined with mine. The temple's sanctity and the outpouring of love from our loved ones served as a testament to the significance of this day, marking the beginning of a beautiful journey as we embarked on our shared path through time and eternity.

As time passed, my parents' hearts embraced Scott with an ever-growing love and acceptance. Being their first daughter, they viewed me as young and cherished, making the prospect of letting me go all the more challenging. Now, having married off our own daughters, my husband and I came to fully understand the depth of their emotions. They were driven by a heartfelt desire to ensure my well-being and happiness not only in this lifetime but for all eternity.

My dad, my ultimate hero, found it particularly difficult to release his first little girl, the same little girl who had once accompanied him during midnight hay harvests, danced on his toes, and held a special place in his heart. The day I left to begin my own journey with Scott, a profound tug on his heart occurred. It was as if a part of his heart, reserved just for me, was deeply affected by my departure. I was his precious little girl, and the love he held for me was immeasurable. As I ventured into a new chapter of life with Scott, I carried with me the unwavering love of my dad, forever grateful for the bond we shared and the cherished memories of being his little girl.

Over the years, my parents' love for Scott blossomed and deepened, nurtured by his unwavering support and willingness to lend a helping hand to my dad whenever needed. It was evident to my father that Scott adored me, treasured me, and made sure I was always taken care of. Witnessing this love and devotion firsthand, my dad's heart was put at ease, knowing that I had found a partner who truly cherished and cared for me. The bond I shared with my parents is an invaluable treasure that I hold close to my heart every single day. I consider myself incredibly fortunate to have been showered with such profound love and affection, especially from my dad, my hero, who exemplified righteousness and faithfulness in every aspect of his life. Their love and support have shaped me into the person I am today, and I will forever be grateful for the extraordinary relationship I share with them.

Reflecting on my journey as a mother, wife, and teacher, I came to recognize the immense blessing of having been raised by a righteous father. Moreover, I felt deeply grateful to have married a man who embodied the same qualities. Scott's devotion to our family was nothing short of extraordinary, and I knew he would have excelled as a stay-at-home dad or a "Mr. Mom." His unwavering presence and support for our children were beyond compare, always there when they needed him, just a phone call away. Whether it was in the bleachers, cheering at their events and games, or encouraging them to pursue their dreams, Scott consistently demonstrated the love and dedication of a truly great father. He proved to be an exceptional parent, particularly in his relationship with our prodigal son Stetsen, meeting him where he was and offering unconditional love and support. Scott's role as a father was unparalleled, earning him the title of the greatest dad ever in my heart.

One afternoon, while sitting with my two youngest daughters, both in their teenage years and radiating confidence, I found myself in awe of the strong and self-assured individuals they had become. In fact, all my children seemed to possess this remarkable sense of confidence and clarity about their values and beliefs. It was a trait I deeply admired as it was something I felt I had not fully achieved myself.

Curious to understand the source of their strength, I asked the girls what experiences or influences in their lives had contributed to shaping them into the incredible individuals they are today. As they shared their stories, I couldn't help but feel a profound sense of pride and gratitude for the unique paths that had led them to become the confident and principled people they are. Their responses filled me with hope and admiration, knowing that the future held so much promise for these remarkable young souls.

Sierra was the first to speak up and simply said, "I know that I am loved by you and Dad. I also know that you and Dad will always be there for me whenever I need it—for the big and small moments and struggles."

Sierra's words resonated deeply within my heart, and her simple yet profound expression of her feelings brought tears to my eyes. As a mother, there is nothing more rewarding than knowing that my daughter feels loved and supported unconditionally. Her unwavering confidence in our presence and our commitment to being there for her through life's ups and downs filled me with immense pride.

Sierra's trust in the strength of our familial bond—where she can turn to us for comfort, guidance, and encouragement in both significant milestones and everyday challenges—is a testament to the foundation of love and security we have built as a family. Hearing her affirmation reaffirmed my dedication to being the best mother I can be, providing my children with the same unwavering love and support that have shaped their confidence and sense of self. Sierra's words served as a poignant reminder of the immense joy and responsibility that come with being a parent and the indescribable fulfillment of knowing that my daughter feels cherished and valued.

Shelby took it one step further. "I know you love me. You are my mom. I was lucky to be raised in a home where love lived, where there was peace." Yes, a good mom moment, but then she added, "I know without a doubt that Dad loves me, that he is always there at the drop of a hat no matter what the circumstances. I know he loves me because he tells me he loves me every time I walk out the door and every night before bed. He assures me every day that I am loved by him." The power of a dad—the power of a righteous, loving dad.

Shelby's heartfelt words filled my heart with overwhelming love and gratitude, affirming the depth of the bond we share as mother and daughter. Her acknowledgment of the love and peace that permeated our home made me realize the impact of creating a nurturing and affectionate environment for our children. As a mother, it was a truly heartwarming moment.

However, Shelby's praise extended even further, emphasizing the extraordinary power of a righteous and loving dad. Her unwavering certainty in her father's love and support showcased the profound influence he had had on her life. His consistent expressions of love, from the moment she walked out the door to the bedtime reassurances, left an indelible mark on her heart. The unwavering presence of a loving and caring father has shaped her sense of security, self-worth, and confidence in the world. The power of a dad's love is immeasurable, and Shelby's words illuminated the significance of a father's role in a child's life, strengthening my appreciation for the incredible man Scott is as both a husband and a father. His love and dedication have truly made an everlasting impact on our children, and I am humbled to witness the transformative power of a righteous and loving dad in shaping our family's foundation of love and support.

In those precious moments of reflection, we allowed the weight of Shelby's words to settle in our hearts. Tears of gratitude flowed freely, affirming the profound impact of Scott's love on each of us. The realization that we were all deeply cherished by our husband and father enveloped us in a warm embrace of love and appreciation. As a family, we basked in the overwhelming love that radiated from his heart. In that intimate space, we felt the presence of Christ's love, knowing that the foundation of love we had diligently nurtured in our home reflected His divine love for each one of us. In that shared moment of vulnerability and joy, we were united by the bond of love that held us together as a family. The love we felt in that instance was a testament to the power of love and the profound impact it has on shaping our lives. Grateful for the gift of our loving husband and father, we cherished the sacred love that connected us all, knowing that it would guide and sustain us through life's journey.

Throughout my years in education, I witnessed firsthand the profound impact a dad has on a child's life. Elder James E. Faust's powerful statement in his April 2001 general conference address resonated deeply with me: "Noble fatherhood gives us a glimpse of the divine attributes of our Father in heaven." As mothers, we fulfill the role of nurturers, offering comfort and care, but a dad's role goes beyond that of a provider. A noble dad takes on the role of protector, answering the call whenever needed and listening to their child's needs with a heart full of love and understanding. Scott exemplified this noble fatherhood, engaging with our children with an open mind and eyes that mirrored the compassion of Christ. His heart of gold served as a shield against the storms of life while allowing our children to explore and learn from their experiences. In the eyes of our children, Scott is a hero, not adorned with superhero symbols or capes, but a hero, nonetheless. His unwavering presence, love, and support have left an indelible mark on our family, shaping us all in profound and meaningful ways.

Reflecting on my journey now thirty-six years later, I remain in awe of the extraordinary relationship I share with my husband, my soulmate, my best friend, and above all, my eternal companion. Pres. Gordon B. Hinckley's counsel rings true in my heart: "Marry the right person in the right place at the right time." For us, the right place was undoubtedly the temple. In Scott, I found the man destined to be by my side. Together, we formed a complete and harmonious union, two halves of a whole. With every fiber of my being, I knew that I had married the man the Lord had prepared specifically for me.

Our love has been an incredible journey, marked by unwavering devotion, trust, and understanding. Scott has been my rock and my anchor, supporting me through life's challenges and rejoicing with me in moments of triumph. As we continue our journey side by side, I am grateful beyond words for the precious gift of his love and companionship, knowing that our bond was divinely orchestrated, and I cherish every moment we share as husband and wife, knowing that our love is eternal.

The last three and a half decades have been a journey filled with both joyous moments and challenging trials, and I won't pretend otherwise, for life is never meant to be a constant stream of happiness. We've faced our share of struggles: financial hardships, parenting challenges, job uncertainties, and relationship hurdles. There was even a time when we separated, a decision I thought was best amidst the financial strain caused by the construction crash in 2009 and the complexities of dealing with our son Stetsen's issues. Scott was seeking a new path for work, and I was exhausted, weary from the uncertainties that plagued us. The arguments over money and our seemingly uncertain future took a toll on us both, leading to the decision to separate.

Yet in that time of reflection, I quickly realized that I needed him by my side, not apart from me. Our bond was resilient, and I discovered that facing life's challenges together was far better than navigating them alone. Our time apart allowed us to catch our breath and reflect, but it also reaffirmed the strength of our love and the deep connection we shared. Through the ups and downs, we've learned that our love is a source of strength, and as we weather life's storms together hand in hand, we find comfort in the knowledge that we are stronger together than apart.

During that challenging period, I confided in a friend who was going through her own divorce, sharing the difficulties my husband Scott and I were facing and my uncertainty about whether we could overcome them. Her response was a profound wake-up call. With unwavering honesty, she looked into my eyes and shared her own experience, saying, "I was happier once he moved out of the house, so if you are truly done with Scott and you are happier with him gone, then stay separated. But if you are miserable without him, then there is still hope that you can work it out."

Her words struck a deep chord within me, forcing me to confront my true feelings. As I pondered her advice, I realized that despite the challenges and struggles, I was far from happier without Scott. In fact, his absence left an emptiness that weighed heavily on my heart. Her words brought clarity to my mind and reaffirmed that our love was worth fighting for. It was a pivotal moment, and I knew that I wanted to make every effort to rebuild and strengthen our relationship. Her wisdom and candor reminded me that hope was not lost and that we still had a chance to work through our difficulties and rediscover the love that had bound us together all those years.

My friend's words hit me like a tidal wave of realization. The truth in her straightforward advice shook me to the core. The time I spent separated from Scott had made one thing abundantly clear: I was miserable without him. The thought of losing the profound connection we shared was unbearable. In that moment, I knew with absolute certainty that I could never live without him by my side. The separation had been a wake-up call, reminding me of the depth of our love and the irreplaceable bond we had nurtured over the years. I was determined to do whatever it took to ensure that we made it through the challenges and came out stronger than ever before. Our love was worth fighting for, and from that point forward, I embraced the commitment to rebuilding our relationship and cherishing the precious connection we shared. The experience had taught me that even in the darkest of times, there was always hope and a chance for growth, and I was resolute in my determination to embrace the journey ahead, knowing that we were stronger together than apart.

Throughout our marriage, my guiding motto has been, "By small and simple things are great things brought to pass" (Alma 37:6). I firmly believe that the foundation of a strong and lasting marriage lies in the simple yet profound acts of love and affection we share every day. From the warmth of a smile to the tenderness of a hug or a sweet "I love you," these gestures form the building blocks of our connection. Our weekly date nights have become a cherished tradition, allowing us to prioritize our relationship and create meaningful memories together. Showing love and appreciation for each other, making the other feel valued and needed, and taking the time to truly listen and talk are essential elements of nurturing our bond. Whether it's enjoying leisurely walks side by side or sharing common hobbies and interests, it's the everyday moments that truly make the difference in our marriage. While grand gestures and big trips may be occasional treats, it is the consistency of the small and simple acts of love that sustain and strengthen the love we share. These daily expressions of affection and thoughtfulness have become the cornerstone of our marriage, filling our lives with happiness and fulfillment, and reminding us that true love is built on the foundation of consistent and genuine care for one another.

As I shifted my perspective and began concentrating on the present instead of constantly looking ahead to the next challenge, a positive transformation took place within our marriage. It was a gradual process, starting with focusing on the little things that we could tackle in the moment rather than fixating on what we lacked or what the future might hold. When disagreements arose about money, we learned to discuss immediate actions to make a positive impact rather than dwelling on what we couldn't attain. Similarly, we approached Stetsen's challenges by addressing them as they arose, embracing the present instead of worrying about what lay ahead. Most importantly, we prioritized each other's needs in our marriage, choosing to put our spouse first.

This shift in perspective allowed us to rediscover the profound power of the small and simple things in our daily lives together.

We learned to cherish each moment and find joy in the everyday expressions of love and care. It became a way of life for us, constantly building and strengthening the foundation of our marriage on these foundational principles. By focusing on the present and embracing the significance of the little things, we have found renewed happiness and unity, proving that the key to a lasting and fulfilling marriage lies in cherishing each moment and continually nurturing the bond we share.

Elder David R. Bednar's powerful statement, "By divine design, men and women are intended to progress together toward perfection and fullness of glory," resonates deeply with me. The phrase "divine design" holds profound significance, emphasizing that marriage is intricately woven into the Lord's eternal plan for us. It is a sacred union meant to provide companionship and support as we journey through life side by side, striving for growth and perfection together. In entering a marriage, we must approach it as true partners, recognizing that neither one is superior or infallible. A successful partnership thrives on shared dreams and passions, with both individuals offering encouragement and support.

Love, at the heart of a Christ-centered home, should be nurtured and cultivated as both partners strive to see each other as Christ sees them. By embracing this divine design, we open ourselves to the transformative power of love and unity, embarking on a shared journey of progress and spiritual growth. Through the lens of a Christ-centered perspective, we find purpose and fulfillment in our roles as eternal companions, working together toward the fullness of glory intended for us by our Heavenly Father.

Elder M. Russell Ballard's counsel regarding the importance of seeking consensus over being right in a marriage resonates deeply with my own experiences. When my husband, Scott, expressed his desire to move to Show Low and purchase a welding supply business, I was initially resistant and reluctant to leave behind our comfortable life in East Mesa. I loved my teaching job and cherished the home we had built. However, I could see that Scott was frustrated with his work and the fast-paced lifestyle of the Metro Phoenix Valley. He believed that owning his own business in Show Low would bring him fulfillment and a sense of purpose.

Despite my hesitation, I recognized the significance of our communication with each other and with Heavenly Father in making such a decision. Rather than prioritizing my desire to stay, I chose to follow Scott, seeking a consensus that would allow us to move forward together. As we communicated openly with each other and with God, the path became clearer, and I began to see the potential and opportunities that awaited us in Show Low.

This experience taught me that in marriage, decisions must be made as a team, valuing each other's perspectives and seeking Heavenly Father's guidance. When we invite God into our discussions and prioritize unity over being right, we create an environment of love and understanding that strengthens our bond as husband and wife.

Looking back, I realized that I initially hesitated to seek the Lord's guidance before moving to Show Low because deep down, I feared the answer I knew I would receive. However, Scott and I took the time to counsel together and ultimately made the decision to relocate. The first few years were challenging as we adjusted to our new surroundings, but as time passed, we came to see that it was indeed a beneficial move for our family. The small town offered unique opportunities that we would not have encountered if we had stayed in Mesa. Our children had the chance to participate in various sports and activities, making teams and pursuing their passions. Our daughter Samantha, in particular, had the chance to showcase her talents in plays she may not have had the opportunity to audition for in a larger high school.

Personally, I also experienced professional opportunities that I would have missed out on if we had remained in Mesa. Our time in Show Low spanned twelve years, and it is filled with cherished memories as well as the lessons we learned from the hardships we faced. Looking back on our journey, I see how seeking the Lord's guidance and embracing change can lead to unexpected blessings and growth for our family.

Inviting God and Christ into our homes is paramount in building a strong and spiritually rooted marriage. We must be open to being guided by the Holy Spirit in every aspect of our lives together. As couples, it is essential to approach decision-making as a unified team, seeking consensus on both significant and minor matters. Whether it involves major life choices such as new job opportunities or relocating or navigating financial challenges, parenting, and other aspects of family life, both partners should be actively engaged in the decision-making process. By seeking the Spirit's guidance and fostering open communication, we can reach agreements that both parties feel at peace with. Embracing this approach strengthens our bond as a couple and reinforces our commitment to building a Christ-centered home. Inviting God and Christ into the heart of our marriage ensures that we walk the path of righteousness, guided by divine principles and united in love and purpose.

As Scott and I wholeheartedly embraced this counsel, the love between us has blossomed and flourished. We have learned to approach decision-making as a team, collaborating and counseling with one another, ensuring that both our minds and hearts remain open to the possibilities before us. Seeking consensus, we then take our choices to the Lord in prayer, acknowledging His hand in every aspect of our lives and decisions. Through this process, I have come to recognize the divine guidance that permeates our marriage.

Inviting the Lord into our eternal union has deepened our bond, providing us with a profound understanding of the changes and decisions we make together. Our commitment to living a Christ-centered life has only strengthened, and with the Lord's help, we continue to build a life filled with love, unity, and purpose. The Lord's presence in our marriage has proven to be a constant source of strength and guidance, inspiring us to walk hand in hand along the path of righteousness and grace.

Legacy, to me, signifies leaving behind a profound and lasting impact, something to be passed down to future generations. My marriage to Scott is a source of immense pride and my most cherished treasure. Our hearts are intertwined, bound together always and forever. In a world where divorce affects so many couples, I am grateful to say that we have stood strong together for thirty-four years and beyond. My deepest wish is that when my posterity speaks of our marriage, they speak of the depth of our love, the way we cherish and support one another, and the dedication we have to fight for our bond. I hope they see the way we walk side by side, working shoulder to shoulder, building a life of love and unity.

My greatest aspiration is that they take our legacy to heart and strive to cultivate the same type of marriage in their own homes. My marriage with my best friend, the person I love most in the world, serves as the foundation of my legacy, and I am determined to leave a legacy of enduring love, strength, and commitment for generations to come.

> Great marriages are built brick by brick,
> day after day, over a lifetime.
>
> —Dieter F. Uchtdorf

Chapter 2

CHILDREN, OH MY!

Whether our home is large or small, it can be a "house of
prayer, a house of fasting, a house of faith, a house of learning,
a house of glory, a house of order, a house of God."
—Doctrine and Covenants 88:119

On September 15, 1988, as I gazed down at my precious newborn
daughter Samantha, a mix of wonder and fear washed over me.
Holding her for the first time, I was in awe of this little life I had
brought into the world, but I was also overwhelmed with apprehension. The weight of responsibility as a mother felt immense raising
her, caring for her, and being the one she would look up to for guidance and love. The title of *mom* held such significance in a child's
life, and I recognized the sacredness of the role. As Elder M. Russell
Ballard stated, "There is no role in life more essential and more eternal than that of motherhood."

At only twenty years old, nearly twenty-one, when Samantha
was born, I was both excited and deeply terrified. Motherhood
brought on a mix of emotions, but the love I felt for my daughter and
the determination to be the best mother I could surpassed any fear.
The journey of motherhood was a roller coaster of challenges, joys,
and unforgettable moments, but one thing was certain: my children
were my greatest blessings and the source of boundless love and fulfillment in my life. Children, oh my!

During the October 2018 general conference, Elder Ronald A. Rasband shared a touching moment about his daughter's concerns regarding bringing children into our challenging world. I found it reassuring to know that even the children of apostles worry about such matters. The sincerity in her heart led her to approach her father with this heartfelt question, knowing he would not judge her and would offer righteous counsel as her protector.

As Elder Rasband addressed the members of the church, his words were filled with emotion, evident in the tears that accompanied his response. He emphatically reassured his daughter and all of us that it is more than okay to bring children into this world. He encouraged us to take heart and stay steadfast on the covenant path, for even though we live in perilous times, we need not fear. His words resonated deeply, reminding us that as we remain faithful and focused on our covenant relationship with God, we can find peace and confidence in the face of uncertainty and challenges.

Growing up in a home where the gospel and the love of Christ were taught, I witnessed the example of my parents, who made it all look so effortless. I count myself fortunate to have been raised in a loving environment with parents who cherished and supported me. My childhood home was built on the foundations of love and hard work, with my three sisters and five brothers forming a close-knit family. From an early age, we were taught the importance of attending church, holding family home evenings, reading scriptures, and offering prayers to our Heavenly Father. All the lessons taught in Primary became an integral part of my life.

However, as time passed, the responsibility of raising a child in a Christ-centered home fell upon my shoulders. By the age of twenty-nine, I was blessed with four children, each one a precious spirit entrusted to my care by God and Christ. Embracing motherhood brought forth a whirlwind of emotions—fear, joy, sadness, happiness, exhaustion—as I navigated through the fulfilling yet challenging days and nights. Nevertheless, I recognized the divine trust placed in me as a mother, and I was determined to raise my children in a righteous home, guided by the love of Christ.

The story of Hagar in the book of Genesis, wandering in the wilderness with her young son, resonates deeply with me. As a mother, I can only imagine her heartache and despair as she faces the harsh reality of having no bread or water to provide for her son. The fear of not being able to save him, to see him suffer and perhaps die, is a mother's worst nightmare. I understand her pain all too well as I, too, experienced the anguish of holding my own son after a devastating accident threatened to take him away from me, not knowing if I would ever see him alive again, praying for a miracle to spare his life.

In the midst of her desperation, an angel brings comfort to Hagar, assuring her that God has heard her son's cries and that they will be sustained. Just as Hagar opened her eyes to find water that would provide for their needs, I, too, witnessed the miraculous intervention of divine help, giving me hope and strength in the most trying times. The story of Hagar reminds me that even in our darkest moments, we can find solace and sustenance through our faith in God's unfailing love and compassion.

As young women, we are raised with the noble goal of becoming righteous mothers in Zion. The family proclamation, issued in 1995, emphasizes the primary responsibility of mothers in nurturing their children. It is a profound and weighty responsibility to nurture young souls. The concept of nurture encompasses a vast array of actions and emotions: caring for, encouraging growth, and fostering development.

Despite having experience in helping to raise my nine younger siblings, I found that motherhood brought its own unique challenges and complexities. It was a humbling journey, and my first step was to ensure that Christ was at the center of our family. Embracing His teachings, love, and guidance, I aspired to create a Christ-centered home where my children could grow, thrive, and become the individuals they were destined to be. Motherhood is a divine calling, and it is through the teachings and example of Christ that I seek to fulfill this sacred role to the best of my ability.

As I pondered the question of how Christ would view my home if He were to walk in through my front door, I couldn't help but feel a sense of trepidation. While the cleanliness of my home didn't concern me, it was the nurturing and encouragement of my children that gave me pause. I yearned for my three daughters to grow into strong and independent individuals, unyielding in the face of worldly pressures and challenges. Similarly, I hoped my son would become a hardworking provider for his future family. The Lord's counsel to teach our children to pray and walk upright before Him (Doctrine and Covenants 68:28) set lofty goals before me. Yet I firmly believed that if Christ were truly present in my home, these aspirations could be achieved. It was both a humbling and empowering realization, knowing that with Christ's guiding influence, I could shape my home into a place of love, learning, and spiritual growth for my children.

When my twelve-year-old daughter approached me, frustrated that she couldn't wear spaghetti-strap shirts like her friends, I couldn't help but chuckle. I vividly remember those camis that were all the rage among her peers. However, I also knew that her school had a strict dress code that prohibited such attire. Explaining this to her, I assured her that it wasn't just her; all her friends were also required to wear T-shirts under their camis to comply with the dress code. While I understood her desire to fit in with her friends, I wanted her to understand the importance of following rules and guidelines even if it meant not being able to wear the latest fashion trends. It was a valuable lesson in respecting authority and making responsible choices, one that I hoped would shape her character as she continued to grow.

As the discussion about modesty and dress code continued with my twelve-year-old daughter, I made sure to emphasize that these rules were not mine but were inspired by the prophets, who asked us to be modest in our attire. Unexpectedly, my four-year-old daughter, who had quietly entered the room, broke into song, singing the Primary song "Follow the Prophets." I couldn't help but smile at this sweet reminder of Christ's presence in our home and in our lives. However, my older daughter reacted differently, telling her younger sister to stop singing the song and then storming off. Yet the message was clear to me: Christ was there, guiding and teaching us through the principles of modesty and obedience to prophetic counsel. In moments like this, I felt a sense of assurance and comfort, knowing that Christ was an ever-present influence, guiding and directing us as a family.

Ah, the teenage years, a roller-coaster ride of emotions and unpredictable behavior. It seemed like my children had transformed into a completely different breed during this phase. Reasoning with them became a challenge as they navigated their way through a sea of emotions. Communication was a struggle, and at times, they seemed like they were from a different planet. The simple and easy Primary lessons on reading scriptures, family prayers, and attending church now became tenfold harder. Although Christ was still present in our home, there were moments when both my children and I found it difficult to see Him amidst the chaos and challenges of adolescence.

Yet even in those trying times, I knew that Christ's love and guidance were ever present, waiting for us to turn to Him with open hearts and minds. As a family, we continued to press forward, navigating the teenage waters together, relying on faith, love, and prayer to guide us through this transformative phase.

Letting go was perhaps the most challenging lesson I had to learn as a mother of teenagers. It meant releasing my expectations and desires and instead, truly listening to them and their hearts. I had to learn to read between the lines and discern their needs and feelings. But the hardest part was resisting the urge to control their every action and decision. I came to understand that their choices and actions were not a reflection of my parenting, and I needed to give them the space to make their own choices even if they were different from what I would have chosen for them. It was a realization that mirrored Satan's plan in the premortal life, where he sought to take away our free agency to ensure we returned safely.

I didn't want to become a stumbling block to my children's growth and development by imposing my will upon them. Instead, I sought to foster an environment of love, trust, and open communication, where they could explore their own paths and learn from their experiences. It was a lesson in humility and faith, trusting that God had a plan for each of my children and that they would find their way with His guidance. As I learned to let go, our relationship deepened, and I witnessed them becoming more confident, independent, and resilient individuals.

Learning this lesson was not a smooth journey, and I carry regrets from some of the moments when I faltered as a mother. I realized that it was crucial to have rules and boundaries in our home, but equally important was being clear about the consequences of breaking those rules with my children. I had to be firm yet fair, consistently outlining the rules and their corresponding consequences. It was a lesson in accountability, teaching my children that every choice they made had an outcome, whether positive or negative. This principle resonated with Christ's plan for us, a plan that emphasized agency and accountability. I hoped that by instilling this understanding in my teenagers, they would see the bigger picture and comprehend the value of making responsible decisions. It was a challenging balance, but through it, we all learned and grew together, with Christ's plan as our guide, leading us toward a brighter and more purposeful path.

In that moment, sitting in my bishop's office with my husband, I felt overwhelmed by my desperation to save my son. My mind was racing, and I was insisting that the bishop intervene, that he talk to my son and force him to attend church and young men's activities. My son had started drifting down a dangerous path, and I felt like I was losing him. I believed that I had to control every aspect of his life, to make him righteous, and to ensure he followed the rules. My thoughts were consumed with *I, I, I, I.* It was a pivotal moment, one that made me realize that my desperate need to control his choices and beliefs was not helping him but rather pushing him further away. I had to come to terms with the fact that I couldn't force righteousness onto him; instead, I needed to be a supportive, loving mother, trusting in God's plan and allowing my son to find his own way back to the path of light and truth.

My sweet, loving bishop, whom I admired and loved, looked me straight in the eye and said words that I will never forget: "I am going to say one thing to you, then I would like you to go home. I can see that Scott does not agree with you. The two of you need to get on the same page, or you will lose your son forever."

Those words hit me like a ton of bricks. They cut straight through my desperation and brought me face-to-face with the reality of the situation. My bishop's gentle-yet-firm guidance made me realize that my approach was pushing my son away instead of drawing him closer. It was a wake-up call that I needed to stop trying to control everything and instead work together with my husband to show our son love, understanding, and support. I needed to let go of my fear and trust in God's plan for our family. It was a difficult lesson to learn, but it marked the beginning of a shift in my parenting approach, one that focused on fostering a loving and open relationship with my son, allowing him the space to find his own path while offering guidance and unconditional love along the way.

That moment in the bishop's office was a turning point for me. It was a painful realization of the mistakes I had made as a mother. I had allowed my fear and desperation to cloud my judgment and had unknowingly been infringing on my son's agency. His words about not being better than Satan stung, but they were a wake-up call that I needed. It was a difficult and humbling process, but I had to confront my own shortcomings and strive to become more Christlike in my approach. I had to learn to trust in God's plan for my son and allow him the space to make his own choices even if they were different from what I had envisioned.

It took time and effort, but gradually, my relationship with my son began to heal. I learned the importance of unconditional love, patience, and understanding. I learned that I needed to be an example of Christ's love rather than trying to control or force his path. It was a lesson I will never forget and one that continues to guide me in my journey as a mother.

As we sit together, my son and I, I can see the frustration in his eyes. He feels that life is unfair, that he is being treated differently from his sisters. I listen to his grievances, trying my best to understand his perspective. It is not easy being a young adult navigating the transition from adolescence to adulthood, and I can see the turmoil he is going through.

As a mother, I want to help him find his way and succeed in life, but I also know that setting boundaries and rules is essential for his growth and development. It is a delicate balance between guiding him and allowing him the freedom to make his own choices and learn from them. I try to explain to him that the rules are not about favoritism or punishment but about teaching responsibility, respect, and accountability. My heart aches as I see the struggle he is going through, but I also know that these challenges are an essential part of his journey toward becoming a responsible and independent adult.

As the night goes on, we talk and share our thoughts, and I hope that our conversation helps him gain a better understanding of why rules are in place and that they come from a place of love and concern. As a mother, my role is to support and guide him even when he doesn't fully comprehend or appreciate the reasons behind the decisions made. I know that in time, he will come to see the value of these lessons and hopefully appreciate the love and care that go into every aspect of our family's life. For now, I will continue to be there for him, to listen, to guide, and to love him unconditionally as we navigate the challenging but rewarding journey of his early adulthood together.

Continuing our discussion, he turns to me and asks, "Do the girls even have a curfew?"

"Of course, they do," I replied. It was a Saturday night, and the curfew for all my children on Saturday was and always had been 11:30 p.m. so that they were in bed before the Sabbath Day started at midnight.

"And what happens if the girls don't get home on time?" Stetsen asked a little smug, goading me into an argument.

As if Christ was sitting there guiding my daughter's home, as soon as he finished the statement, in walk the two girls. It was only 10:00 p.m., and they were home early. I greeted the girls as they walked through the door, "Hey, guys, why are you home so early?"

They stated that they ran out of things to do and decided to come home. I looked at my son and asked, "You were saying?"

He solemnly shook his head, shocked that the girls had come home when they ran out of things to do, so I asked him, "What did you do when you ran out of things to do on a Saturday night?"

As a mother, I had to come to terms with the fact that my son Stetsen was his own person with his own choices and decisions to make. Despite my efforts to teach him and set boundaries, he seemed to be testing the limits more than his sisters did. It was difficult to see him making choices that I knew could lead to trouble and heartache, but I also realized that he needed the space to learn and grow on his own.

The lesson I had to learn was to let go of my need to control every aspect of his life and trust that the values and principles we had taught him would guide him in the right direction. It was not easy to watch him stay out late, engage in questionable activities, and seemingly disregard the rules we had in place. However, I had to remind myself that he was his own person, and ultimately, he would be responsible for the consequences of his actions.

Letting go and allowing him to make his own choices were two of the hardest things I had to do as a mother, but they were also essential for his growth and development. I had to have faith that the lessons we had taught him throughout his life would eventually take root and guide him back to the right path. As he navigated through the challenges of young adulthood, I could only hope that he would come to understand the importance of responsibility and accountability and choose a path that would lead him to a fulfilling and successful life.

Meeting teenagers where they are became a pivotal lesson in my journey as a parent. Like Christ, who showed up for those in need, I learned to be there for my children in their times of struggle and uncertainty. This lesson was especially crucial during the teenage years when they faced unique challenges and emotions. Instead of trying to force my own agenda or expectations upon them, I sought to listen, understand, and support them. Just as Christ ministered to individuals according to their needs, I discovered that each of my children required a different approach. Some needed more guidance and structure while others needed space to explore and make their own decisions. By trusting the promptings of the Spirit, I was guided to be present when they needed me most, to offer a listening ear, a shoulder to cry on, or advice when they sought it. Meeting my children where they were and being a constant source of love and support allowed them to navigate through their teenage years with greater confidence and trust in themselves.

It is close to ten thirty at night, and my youngest, Sierra, still has not gone to sleep. I see her light under her door. She is my sleeper. It is rare that she makes it past 9:00 p.m. each night, especially on a school night, but this night, she is awake. Only the two of us are at home. Scott is working nights, and the other three are raised and gone. The house is quiet, except for Sierra. I knock on the door and go on in. She is sitting there; her countenance is cloudy. The look on her face is something I had seen many times, so I ask her, "Do we need to talk?"

She simply nods her head as her eyes swell up with tears. Even though it is late and I must get up early the next morning, we talk. As I sit down next to Sierra, I can sense that something is bothering her. She begins to share her thoughts and feelings with me, opening up about the pressures and anxieties she's been facing lately. As her mother, my heart aches for her, but I know that this moment is crucial for our relationship. I listen attentively, offering a safe space for her to express herself. In the silence that follows, I wrap my arms around her, assuring her that I am here for her no matter what.

We talk late into the night, discussing her fears, hopes, and dreams. In this tender moment, I recognize the importance of being present for my children and meeting them where they are even in the late hours of the night. I understand that being a mother means being there for them in times of joy and sorrow, helping them navigate the ups and downs of life with love and support. This intimate conversation with Sierra strengthens our bond and reminds me of the eternal significance of motherhood. It is in these moments that I feel the love of Christ guiding me as I strive to be the mother my children need. Christ meets us where we are, so we must do the same as mothers in Zion.

The final huge lesson I learned about raising children is to open our homes and hearts to the children around us—to those in need of Christ in their lives, to those in need of role models, to those in need of a safe refuge from the storms raging in their lives and their homes.

As a professional educator, I have always considered myself a collector of children. I have hundreds of children who have walked in and out of my life: students both young and old, my children's friends, young women, girls I coached in soccer, and so many more. I designed my classroom and administrative office as a place of refuge, a place where my students felt peace. I became an advocate for so many children over the years. My home was already set up with Christ as the center. My children's friends were always around. Getting ready for Friday night football games, game nights, parties, movie nights—my home was a place of refuge.

In opening our hearts and homes to the children around us, we create a haven where they can feel accepted, loved, and valued. As a teacher and a mother, I have come to understand that being a collector of children is a sacred responsibility. Each child who enters my life brings with them unique experiences and challenges. My classroom and home have become safe spaces where these young souls can find solace from the storms of life. I have witnessed troubled teenagers searching for direction, finding comfort in the support and guidance provided in my home. Our family's Christ-centered foundation has allowed us to offer genuine love and understanding to those in need. We welcome my children's friends and my students, creating an environment of acceptance and warmth. These experiences have taught me that motherhood extends beyond my immediate family, embracing a broader community of young hearts that need the love of Christ in their lives. As we open our homes and hearts to others, we fulfill our divine purpose to love and care for God's children.

It is Friday night. The big-rivalry high school football game is tonight. My daughters are cheerleaders, so there is a lot of movement and excitement throughout the house. Girls are doing hair and makeup. The boys stop by to eat the pizza stacked up in the kitchen. Laughter rings out. Songs break out. Everyone is happy to be together, happy to be in my home.

One young lady comes and sits down next to me. She turns to me with a look of amazement in her eyes and says, "Your home is always so peaceful. I can feel the peace every time I walk through your door."

I start looking around me at the laughter, singing, the downing of pizza, and wondering how she can think that this is peaceful. As I examine her face, I can see that she feels Christ in our home. My heart swells with love for this young lady as I put my arms around her and give her a quick hug. I can see that she can feel the peace that only Christ can bring into a home. Her own home far from peaceful. I knew she had found peace and refuge in my home, as did so many other young men and women throughout the teenage years.

In that moment, I felt a deep sense of gratitude and fulfillment as I realized the impact my home had on others. It wasn't just the excitement of the football game or the fun of being with friends that made my home special but rather the underlying atmosphere of peace and love that permeated every corner. As a mother and educator, I had striven to create an environment where all who entered could feel the love of Christ and experience a sense of calm amidst the chaos of the world. This young lady's words affirmed that my efforts had not been in vain. It was a reminder of the power of a Christ-centered home and the far-reaching effects it could have on the hearts of those who walked through its doors. I treasured this moment, knowing that my home had become a refuge for others, just as it had been for my own family.

As the nest gradually empties, I find myself cherishing the memories of those bustling Friday nights, the laughter-filled conversations, and the vibrant energy of youth who once filled every corner of my home. Each of these young souls brought their unique presence and left an indelible mark on my heart. Their departures may leave a void, but I hold on to the peace and joy they brought into my life. Their presence in my home was a testament to the importance of opening our hearts and doors to others, and I am grateful for the relationships we built with these remarkable young people. Even as they venture out into the world, I know that a part of my home's spirit will forever accompany them on their journey. My home may be quieter now, but the memories of these beautiful connections continue to resonate in my heart, reminding me of the profound impact we can have on others simply by offering love, acceptance, and Christlike refuge.

As I embrace the role of a grandmother, I find myself filled with indescribable joy. Seeing my family expand and witnessing my children becoming parents have brought a profound sense of fulfillment and love into my life. The bond of love I have for my family continues to deepen, becoming an everlasting and eternal force centered in the love of my Savior.

Now, my focus is on keeping Christ at the center of my home not only for my children but also for my precious grandchildren. When they walk through my doors, I want them to feel the warmth and love of their Savior enveloping them. These invaluable lessons I have learned throughout my journey as a mother and grandmother are etched in my heart and soul, and I strive to pass them on through both my words and actions.

With Christ as our guide, I am confident that the legacy of love and faith will be carried on through generations to come. The following poem by C. C. Miller, titled "The Echo," illustrates the importance, influence, and impact parents have on their children:

'Twas a sheep, not a lamb

That strayed away in the parable Jesus told,

A grown-up sheep that strayed away

From the ninety and nine in the fold.

And why for the sheep should we seek.

And earnestly hope and pray?

Because there is a danger when sheep go wrong:

They lead the lambs astray.

Lambs will follow the sheep, you know.

Wherever the sheep may stray.

When sheep go wrong,

It won't take long till the lambs are as wrong as they.

And so with the sheep, we earnestly plead.

For the sake of the lambs today,

For when the sheep are lost

What a terrible cost

The lambs will have to pay.[1]

---

[1] C. C. Miller, "The Echo," in *Best-Loved Poems of the LDS People*, ed. Jack M. Lyon and others (1996), 312–13.

Leaving a legacy of building and raising my children in a Christ-centered home is my most cherished aspiration. It is the foundation that Scott and I have diligently laid for our children and others who seek refuge, peace, and most importantly, Christ. This Christ-centered home serves as a haven where love and faith flourish and where my children can find the strength to face life's challenges. My greatest hope is for my children to embrace this legacy and carry it forward, passing it on to their own families. A legacy of being raised in a Christ-centered home is a gift beyond measure, one that I pray will endure through generations, guiding each soul to the light and love of our Savior.

A HOME THAT IS FOUNDED ON
Faith
IS A HOME IN WHICH
Jesus Christ
IS CONSIDERED DAILY.
A HOME WHERE
His voice
CAN BE HEARD.

—Emily Belle Freeman

Chapter 3

MY PRODIGAL SON

When There's Nowhere Else To Run
Is There Room For One More Son.
—Robert D. Hales

I stand at the gate with a heart full of hope and love, ready to welcome my son back into my arms. As a mother, it is my unwavering duty to wait patiently, to never give up on him, and to believe in the goodness that lies within him. The journey has been tumultuous, filled with moments of joy and heartache, but I know that deep within him, the light of his true self still shines.

There are days when I catch a glimpse of that glimmer, a flicker of the boy I raised, and it fills me with renewed hope. I know he is fighting battles of his own, facing challenges I cannot fully comprehend, but I will never stop standing at the gate, yearning for the day when he returns. My love for my son knows no bounds, and I will remain steadfast, praying for his safe journey home. Someday, I believe he will find his way back, and I will be here, arms open wide, ready to embrace him once more. Until then, I stand at the gate, watching, hoping, and loving him unconditionally.

As a mother, watching my son take his own path, much like the prodigal son, has been a heart-wrenching experience. Just as the father in the parable, I had to come to terms with the fact that my son needed to explore life on his terms even if it meant going astray.

I knew I couldn't force him to follow the path I had envisioned for him. It was his life, his choices, and his journey to undertake.

However, like the father in the story, my love and hope for my son never wavered. I watched him venture down dark alleys and stumble upon treacherous roads, and every time, my heart ached with worry. But I never stopped praying for his safe return, standing at the gate of hope, longing for the day he would find his way back. Just as the father in the story embraced his prodigal son with open arms, I eagerly await the moment when my son comes home. For now, I stand at the gate, a beacon of love and understanding, ready to welcome him back when he is ready to return.

The reunion of the prodigal son with his father is a powerful moment filled with love, forgiveness, and redemption. It mirrors the longing in my heart as a mother, waiting for my son to come home. When that day finally arrives and I see my son coming down the path, my heart will leap with joy just like the father in the parable. I will run to embrace him, showing him the same compassion and love that never wavered during his absence. Like the prodigal son, my son may feel unworthy of my unconditional love, but I will remind him that he was lost and is found again. Those words will be music to my ears as I see my son return to the place where he belongs, in the embrace of a mother who never stopped hoping, praying, and waiting for his safe return. In that moment, all the pain and heartache will fade away, replaced by the joy of reunion and the knowledge that my son is home, and he is found again.

The journey of carrying Stetsen in my womb was undoubtedly the most challenging of all my pregnancies. From the very beginning, I faced complications, experiencing constant bleeding and severe morning sickness that made it impossible to keep any food down. At just twenty-eight weeks, I went into early labor and was dilated to a four, prompting the doctor to prescribe strict bed rest. For the next eleven weeks, I had to stay still, confined to bed, while my two-year-old played around me. It felt like an eternity, the longest and most trying nine months of my life. Each day, I held on to hope and prayed for a safe delivery, knowing that the end result would be the arrival of my precious son, but the journey was a true test of patience, strength, and faith.

The early morning of March 10, 1991, marked the moment I went into labor, and it was a terrifying experience. As I was getting ready to leave, my water broke suddenly, prompting us to rush to the hospital just a few miles away. Within a matter of minutes after arriving at the delivery room, Stetsen was born, the entire process taking less than twelve minutes. However, his rapid entrance into the world caused some breathing difficulties, and the medical team quickly took him to the nursery for observation. Scott, my husband, was by his side while they attended to me. The whirlwind of emotions on that day, from fear and urgency to relief and joy, made it a momentous occasion that I will never forget.

After Scott and Stetsen returned from the nursery, it was clear that everything was fine with his lungs, and he was in perfect health. As I cradled him in my arms for the first time, an overwhelming feeling of love washed over me. His delicate pale skin, tiny fingers, and toes were a marvel to behold. I was filled with gratitude that this beautiful soul had safely entered my life. Stetsen had completely captured my heart.

Throughout his infancy, he proved to be a delightful baby, always seeking cuddles and communicating with me in his own adorable way. Although he didn't start talking in full sentences until he was two, he had a unique way of expressing himself. It was Samantha, his older sister, who did most of the talking for him during his early years. At two, he started speaking in full sentences, and I was touched when his first word turned out to be *hat*, an amusing coincidence since he was named after one.

From a young age, it was evident that Stetsen had a natural affinity for sports. Even as a fussy baby, I found solace in putting him in his seat next to the TV and turning on a golf tournament, which seemed to calm him down. As a toddler, he always had a ball in his hand, regardless of its type. At the age of five, we enrolled him in Little League, and his talent on the field quickly became apparent. By the time he was eight, he was playing on the major league teams with boys who were much older.

Stetsen's passion for baseball continued to grow, but it also came with some unintended consequences. At around ten years old, when we decided to sell our house, we had to replace several windows that had been cracked and broken by Stetsen's powerful baseball throws. There were four windows that were fully cracked and another two with small cracks that needed replacement before the house could be sold. While it was an expense, it was a testament to his dedication to the sport and his impressive arm strength.

As I watched my twelve-year-old son Stetsen pass the sacrament for the first time after being ordained a deacon, my heart swelled with pride. He had always been such a sweet and loving boy with a passion for sports like baseball, soccer, and diving. Outdoors was his playground, and he loved camping, hunting, and spending time with his dad.

Stetsen brought so much joy to my life; he was always smiling and had a special bond with me, his momma. He was my own stripling warrior, a strong and faithful young man who stood by my side always. When he was little, he never strayed too far from my side, and I cherished those moments when he would snuggle up to me, finding comfort in my embrace. My only son, my little boy, held my heart in his hands, and being with him was pure happiness.

Stetsen's determination to earn his Eagle Scout award before turning fourteen was a testament to his drive and ambition. He wanted to outdo his dad, Scott, who had achieved the same honor at a slightly older age. Growing up surrounded by three sisters, Stetsen often teased that he lived in a house of pink, but he cherished his sisters, especially his advocate and best friend Shelby. With his infectious grin and charm, Stetsen could easily win us over, and he knew just how to get what he wanted.

As he sailed through his preteen years, he brought joy and laughter to everyone around him. Playing games, spending time together, and showering him with love were always a delight. Stetsen had a mischievous side too, and he took pleasure in sneaking up on his sisters and me, causing us to scream with surprise. His love for scaring us became a cherished memory of his playful nature.

As Stetsen entered high school, his life took a different turn. His passion for soccer led him to make the varsity squad as a freshman, which filled us with pride and excitement. However, along with his success came a change in his social circle. He started spending time with a group of friends who were not a positive influence on him. It became evident that Stetsen had a follower personality, easily swayed by the dominant individuals within the group.

As time passed, we learned that his assistant soccer coach had introduced him to harmful behaviors, including exposure to pornography. My heart broke as I watched my son transform into someone unrecognizable, far from the sweet and happy boy he once was. The challenges he faced in high school were difficult for both him and our family, and it became our mission to help him find his way back to the path of goodness and positivity.

As Stetsen's behavior continued to spiral, I could still see glimmers of the good-hearted boy he used to be, but they were fading fast. He became someone who would sneak out at night to meet his questionable friends, and his school attendance suffered as he started skipping classes. His resistance to going to church grew stronger, and he felt like everyone there was against him, causing him to withdraw even further. His once bright and cheerful countenance turned dark and solemn, making it difficult for me to recognize the son I knew so well. He seemed distant and disconnected from our family, including his sisters and even from Scott and me. It broke my heart to see my sweet son slipping away from us, lost in a world that I couldn't seem to reach.

The day of Stetsen's accident in 2007 is etched forever in my memory, haunting me with its painful images. I can still see him on that stretcher, being rushed into the helicopter bound for Scottsdale, with the grim words echoing in my ears that he might not survive the journey. I was told I should say my goodbyes as it might be the last time I ever saw him alive. That dark day in August shook me to the core, but it also brought forth incredible miracles and answers to our prayers. Amidst the darkness, there was a glimmer of hope that Stetsen might find his way back to the gospel, that he might want to return to the fold and come back down the path where I was standing at the gate, waiting and hoping for his return.

Within a year after the accident, Stetsen seemed to forget the countless miracles that had unfolded in his life. He forgot the profound impact of the priesthood blessings, the prayers that had been fervently offered, and the divine protection that allowed him to survive the car accident with only a few scars to show for it. The doctors diagnosed him with a traumatic brain injury (TBI), a condition he would carry with him throughout his life. While he was considered lucky to have regained 90 percent of his abilities and memories, the TBI still left its mark.

Despite the challenges, he remained resilient and continued to pursue his dreams. However, the fear of losing him never left me, and I couldn't help but try to control every aspect of his life, desperate to keep him close. Yet my efforts were pushing him further away, and I began to realize that my controlling nature was driving a wedge between us. It has been fourteen years since that life-changing event, and I still stand at the gate, waiting, hoping, and praying that he will return completely, finding his way back to the path we once walked together.

Stetsen's decision to join the military right after high school was a moment filled with mixed emotions for me. I agreed to support his choice but with a condition: he had to join the reserves, as I still hoped he would serve a mission. Looking back, I realized I was trying to control his life, impose my desires on him, and deny him his agency. I was being unfair and preventing him from pursuing his own dreams, forcing him to follow mine. But life has its own way of teaching us lessons, and within a year of his graduation, Stetsen turned nineteen and decided to turn in his mission papers. I was filled with hope and excitement, only to be heartbroken when he chose not to serve a mission. My disappointment and embarrassment clouded my judgment, and I had to once again confront the fact that this was not about me; it was about Stetsen and his path in life. I had to let go of my expectations and learn to support him unconditionally.

During the following years, I wish I could say that I had completely changed the way I treated and dealt with my son, but the truth is I was still struggling. I desperately wanted him to choose the righteous path I envisioned for him, and I found myself pushing and trying to control his decisions. Our relationship was strained, and there were numerous arguments. There were times when I didn't even know where Stetsen was or whom he was with, leaving me filled with worry and fear for his well-being. These were truly dark years for both of us, and I was still grappling with how to let go of my need for control and learn to love and support him unconditionally no matter what path he chose.

During this challenging period of my life, I could sense my family beginning to fall apart. My two younger daughters still needed my love and support, but there were times when I couldn't be there for them as I should have been. My oldest daughter, Samantha, was starting her own family, and I felt like I was failing her by not being the supportive mother she needed. My husband and I argued constantly over what to do about Stetsen, and those arguments eventually led to our separation and growing apart. In my heart, I blamed him for the problems we were facing, believing that if only he had listened to me and chosen my way, everything would be okay.

Once again, I was making it all about me and not about him. I was losing my son, not to death but by forcing my desires onto him and denying him the freedom to make his own choices. I was taking away his agency, and in doing so, I was aligning myself more with Satan's plan than with Christ's teachings of love and agency. It was a painful realization but one that helped me understand that I needed to change my approach and let go of control to truly support and love my son as Christ would have me do.

During a tumultuous period when Stetsen was around twenty-one years old, we endured six months of not knowing his whereabouts or if he was safe. It was a harrowing time for our family as we desperately searched for him, but he seemed to have vanished without a trace. Both Scott and I tirelessly looked for him, but all our efforts yielded no results. There were rumors that he had been spotted living in the woods, surviving off the land, or residing in his car, but nobody could provide specific details of his location. Those were some of the darkest days of my life.

Years later, I mustered the courage to ask Stetsen about that period, hoping to understand what he had gone through, but all he would say was that I did not want to know. The pain of those lost months still lingers in my heart, but I have come to realize that there are some things beyond our control and understanding.

During that challenging period, I embarked on a soul-searching journey, delving deep into my innermost thoughts and emotions. I confronted the harsh reality of my actions toward my sweet son and acknowledged that his choices did not define my worth as a mother. It was a time of introspection, realizing that God had entrusted these precious children to Scott and me, and our responsibility was to instill in them a foundation rooted in Christ and then allow them to chart their own paths. I faced my shortcomings and relinquished the idea that controlling my son was the solution. Humbling myself, I turned to my loving Heavenly Father in heartfelt prayer, seeking forgiveness, guidance, and strength. Above all, I prayed for my son's well-being and that the damaged relationship between us could be repaired. My prayers have persisted to this day, yearning to see Stetsen through God's eyes and earnestly hoping for reconciliation and forgiveness.

During that transformative period, my perspective on my son underwent a profound shift. I came to realize that he was now a grown man, and I needed to release my grip and allow him to forge his own path in life. I learned to meet Stetsen where he was, respecting his journey and choices rather than imposing my desires upon him. As I let go of my preconceived expectations, I began to see the beautiful innate qualities he possessed, the righteous traits that were an integral part of his being. I marveled at his strong sense of service and compassion, his innate ability to reach out to those in need and champion the underprivileged. Focusing on the Christlike qualities within him, my perception of my son became crystal clear, aligning with how Christ and God saw him. My love for him grew immeasurably, reigniting the fond memories of my sweet little boy, whose smile had always been a source of solace and joy in my life.

Throughout the years of navigating the challenges posed by a wayward son, I have often been asked if I wish he had never strayed. While it may seem tempting to wish for a smoother path, I cannot deny the profound lessons I have learned through this journey with my prodigal son. These experiences have shaped me into the person I am today. The most crucial lesson I have gained is the importance of allowing our children to determine their own paths and inheritances in life. It involves granting them the freedom to explore, build their testimonies, and make their own choices. I have come to understand the immense value of respecting their agency and learning to emulate Christ's love and understanding instead of trying to control or force them into a mold. As difficult as it has been, I now cherish the opportunity to witness my son's growth and development as he charts his own course, soaring to new heights on his own terms.

Today, after fifteen years, Stetsen continues to serve in the military, staying true to the path he set out on all those years ago. Although he didn't serve a mission for the church, he found his own meaningful mission within the military. Stetsen has proven himself to be an exceptional soldier, dedicated and hardworking, always ready to support and uplift those around him. He is the one his commanding officers turn to when someone needs help or guidance. Instead of leading from above, he stands side by side with his comrades, leading by example and serving with honor.

Stetsen's chosen path is righteous and honorable, and he has not strayed from the foundation of the gospel. Despite the challenges he faced, he remains a good man, knowing that God and Christ love him. I couldn't be prouder of the person he has become and the path he has chosen.

Yes, I still hope and pray that my son will return to the fold, to embrace his blessings and covenants once again. I have faith that he will find his way back, as I know the goodness and light are still within him. For now, I will patiently stand at the gate, waiting for him to choose the path that leads back to me. As Elder Jeffrey R. Holland beautifully expressed, "I know that if we will be faithful, there is a perfectly tailored robe of righteousness ready and waiting for everyone."[2] I firmly believe that there is such a robe of righteous-

---

[2] Jeffrey R. Holland, "The Other Prodigal," General Conference, April 2002.

ness waiting for my son, my prodigal son, when he is ready to come home.

Yes, I stand by the gate, just like the father in the parable of the Prodigal Son, waiting, hoping, and filled with anticipation for the day my child will return. My heart yearns to rush to their side, to embrace them with love and forgiveness, to welcome them home with open arms, just as Christ and our Heavenly Father welcome us back with love and mercy when we turn to them.

I strive to pass on the legacy of unconditional love and patience, teaching my children the importance of waiting at the gate no matter how long it takes, ready to receive them with open hearts when they choose to come back. For in the end, the love of a parent can be a guiding light, helping our children find their way back home.

The difference between mercy and grace? Mercy gave the prodigal son a second chance. Grace gave him a feast.

—Max Lucado

You can read the entire story of Stetsen's accident in Dr. Stephanie West's book *A Mother's Journey, a Family Changed Revisited*, available through Amazon.

Chapter 4

Grown Children and Grandchildren

Therefore, shall a man leave his father and his mother, and
shall cleave unto his wife: and they shall be one flesh.
—Genesis 2:24

Once a mom, always a mom. The dream of having a house filled with my grown children, their spouses, and grandchildren laughing and sharing love around the dining-room table has been a beacon of hope for me through the challenging teenage years. While raising teenagers was undoubtedly tough, I had envisioned that the grown-children stage would be smoother and more carefree. However, reality has taught me otherwise.

As my children have grown into adults, new challenges have arisen, and the dynamics have shifted. Navigating the complexities of adult relationships, balancing their independence with my desire to be involved, and respecting their autonomy while still offering support have proven to be both rewarding and occasionally heart-wrenching. Nevertheless, the dream of that warm, loving gathering around the table remains a cherished aspiration, reminding me that no matter the stage, my role as a mother continues to be one of love, guidance, and unwavering support.

To date, I have been blessed with three wonderful sons-in-law, one amazing daughter-in-law, and nine precious grandchildren, whom I adore with all my heart. Welcoming new members into our family brought both joy and apprehension as we navigated the blending of new ideas and personalities. My heart swelled with love as I gained more sons, yet I grappled with the challenge of giving them the space to grow and establish their own identities alongside my daughters. It was a delicate balance between being a supportive mother and allowing them the freedom to chart their own paths.

As my children became adults, I learned the importance of giving them the room to make decisions and the trust to handle their lives independently. Recognizing that my role as their mother had shifted from being the guiding force to being a source of love and encouragement, I embraced the process of letting go and allowing them to take charge of their own lives. It has been a journey of learning and growth for all of us, filled with beautiful moments and the realization that our family's love and connection remain strong despite the changing dynamics.

As I reflect on those cherished moments of tucking my little ones into bed, I am filled with both nostalgia and pride in the incredible adults they have become. The joy of knowing they are now creating their own families and homes is immeasurable. Witnessing them raise their own children with the values we instilled in them brings a profound sense of fulfillment. Through the years, my children have taught me invaluable lessons about motherhood and life. They have shown me the true meaning of unconditional love, patience, and resilience. They have inspired me to be a better mother, to listen more attentively, and to support them unconditionally as they pursue their dreams and aspirations. The journey of motherhood is a never-ending process of growth, and I am grateful for the opportunity to continue learning and evolving alongside my remarkable children. Their love and presence have enriched my life beyond measure, and I am forever proud to be their mother.

It was disheartening to realize that my vision of being the beloved mother-in-law wasn't as simple as I had hoped. Despite my efforts to emulate the loving examples set by my own mother and mother-in-law, my family didn't always come together as I had envisioned. Sunday dinners, family outings, and gatherings for special occasions seemed to fall short of uniting everyone consistently. At times, I felt a pang of disappointment, wondering if I was doing something wrong or if my dream of a tightly knit, loving family was unrealistic.

However, I came to understand that each person's life journey is unique, and the dynamics of family relationships are ever evolving. Instead of trying to control the outcome, I began to cherish the moments when my family did come together, whether big or small, appreciating the connections we made during those times. I learned to accept that my role as a mother-in-law was not about achieving a picture-perfect vision but about offering love, support, and understanding to each family member in their own individual way.

The anticipation and excitement leading up to the family reunion at Bear Lake in 2019 were palpable. Scott and I had meticulously planned every detail, from the rented cabin on the hill to the array of activities and delicious food awaiting us. As the Fourth of July weekend approached, my heart swelled with joy, envisioning the unforgettable memories we would create together. It was an opportunity for all of us to strengthen our bonds and forge lasting connections with each other. I couldn't wait to see the grandchildren playing together, getting to know each other better, and creating a tapestry of cherished moments. This family reunion was more than just a gathering; it was meant to become a tradition that would bring us closer together for years to come.

Reflecting on the family reunion at Bear Lake brings mixed emotions, and I can't help but smile at my grand plans that went awry. The reality of the run-down cabin and its limited space quickly became apparent, and I felt disheartened by the complaints and discomfort that emerged. My vision of a united, harmonious gathering seemed shattered as each member pursued their own interests, and the lack of common activities left me feeling disheartened. The generational gaps became evident as the grown boys immersed themselves in video games, leaving the younger children feeling left out. The disconnect in our activities and the inability to share meaningful experiences as a family left me wondering where we had gone wrong. Despite my best intentions, it seemed that the family reunion fell short of becoming the cherished tradition I had envisioned.

In my frustration and disappointment, Scott and I decided to call a family counsel on the last night of the reunion. Hoping to salvage some positive aspects, we began by asking what they liked about the gathering, only to be met with awkward silence and forced responses. My emotions got the better of me, and I expressed my frustration, reminding them of the effort and resources we had invested in planning the reunion. I then proceeded to lay out my expectations for the future, hoping that a clear directive would ensure their participation and enthusiasm. I outlined a strict schedule, demanding their presence at Sunday dinners, Christmas Eve fondue, and future family reunions, all with the hope of fostering a united family bond. In my attempt to create a sense of togetherness, I had inadvertently pushed them away with my forceful demands, which only added to the growing divide between us.

In the aftermath of that family counsel, emotions ran high. My daughters were upset, one even leaving the room, while the sons-in-law were unsure how to react. The grandchildren were spared from witnessing the tension as they were asleep, and I felt relieved about that. Yet I couldn't help but feel the weight of my mistakes. I knew I had handled the situation poorly and that my desire to be the favorite, the center of everyone's attention, had clouded my judgment. I wanted my family to naturally come together, to share love and joy, but my forceful demands only pushed them further away.

I retreated to my bedroom, where tears flowed, knowing this was one of my worst moments as a mother. I yearned for their love and acceptance, but I had to recognize that love is not something that can be demanded or forced; it must be nurtured and freely given. It was a serious wake-up call, a stark reminder that being a mom means learning and growing alongside my children and that true love comes from letting go and allowing them to choose their own paths.

Within a week of returning home from California, my daughter Shelby approached me, just as I expected. Shelby has always been the peacemaker, wise in her words and the one my youngest seeks advice from. I could tell that my other children had spoken to her, and now it was her turn to set me straight in her unique way. "Mom, we really need to talk," she said firmly.

I replied, "Yes, we do." I knew I had made mistakes, but I didn't know how to fix them or how to be the favorite, the one everyone wanted to be around. I doubted if I ever could be that person.

Shelby continued, her words hitting home, "You need to let go and not be so demanding of our time. You raised us to be independent and taught us how to run our own homes. You've done well, but now we have families of our own. It's our time to build our own family traditions. It doesn't mean we won't come and see you, but you need to find a way to do it on our terms and not yours."

Her words stung a bit, but I knew she was right. We sat and talked for a while, coming up with a better plan together. I realized that I needed to invite them and then step back, hoping they would come on their own terms. It was time to respect their independence and allow them to choose when and how they wanted to be together as a family.

This experience taught me valuable lessons. The first was to meet my children where they were at in their lives. Just like when they were teenagers, each of my adult children was dealing with their own unique challenges in their own families. I had been too focused on myself, and it was time to shift my perspective to be more about them. Shelby's advice to invite instead of demanding was wise. I needed to open my doors and let them know they were welcome whenever they could come. I could still plan activities, but I had to involve everyone and not do it all for them. It was important to let them take part and plan for their own families. While they cherished our family traditions, they also needed time to create their own. I had to meet them where they were and respect their journey.

The way I interacted with my grown children started to evolve in the days, months, and years that followed. I realized that I could extend invitations to family events, but I had to be content if they chose not to come, so I began planning for our first Sunday family dinner each month. We gathered at 4:00 p.m., a time that worked well for everyone after church, meetings, and nap times for the little ones. I carefully prepared meals that I knew they all enjoyed. As time went on, we even welcomed others in need to join us at these gatherings, like missionaries, single parents without nearby family, and other extended family members. The atmosphere was relaxed with no pressure to attend.

To my delight, these family dinners have become cherished occasions, eagerly anticipated by everyone. We laugh, talk, and share memories, and it has become a precious time for building bonds and expressing our love for one another. These regular gatherings have become the highlight of our month, providing us with an opportunity to strengthen our family ties and make lasting memories together. I have come to understand that meeting my children where they are—always—is crucial in maintaining our close and loving relationship.

The second important lesson my grown children have taught me is the value of low-key and easy-to-plan family reunions. They have shown me that trying to convince them to go to far-off destinations is challenging. Instead, we have discovered that the most enjoyable and successful family trips are those close by, where everyone feels comfortable and at ease. Our old hometown in the scenic White Mountains of Arizona has become one of our favorite reunion spots. It's easily accessible, and we all know the area well. There, we have our favorite restaurants to visit and plenty of friends and family to connect with. We extend invitations, hoping they will come, but we also understand if they cannot. Regardless, we proceed with the plan, and the gatherings have turned into wonderful memories filled with hikes, fireside chats, snowfall watching, and delicious meals prepared together. These stress-free reunions last no more than a few days but leave us with a wealth of cherished experiences and strengthened family bonds. My children have taught me that simplicity and familiarity are the key ingredients to successful family gatherings.

In the early years after my daughters got married, I found myself constantly keeping track of holiday schedules and fretting over how much time they spent with their in-laws. It was a source of immense stress, and I would feel hurt if they didn't spend all their time with me. I yearned to be their favorite, failing to realize the unfairness of such expectations. This was a lesson that took time to learn and even more time to figure out how to handle gracefully. I had to come to terms with the fact that I might not see all my children at once during the holidays and learn to be okay with that reality. I had to understand that they were now part of new families with their own traditions and obligations and that I couldn't expect them to revolve their lives solely around me. It was a challenging lesson, but it eventually led me to embrace a more flexible and understanding approach to family gatherings, one that valued quality time spent together rather than a rigid adherence to schedules.

After years of feeling disappointed and upset during holidays, I finally found an approach that works for me. Just as I do for family reunions and dinners, I plan a special meal for every holiday—Easter, Thanksgiving, Christmas, New Year's Day—and for the summer holidays, I organize barbecues and outdoor activities. Then I extend invitations to my children and let them decide if they can make it. The key is that I must be okay if they cannot come.

I've learned to let go of expectations and to cherish the time we do get to spend together. I only ask that they inform me a few days in advance if they're coming so I can prepare enough food. You might think this approach won't work, that no one will show up, but surprisingly, I now have more visits from my children than ever before. By giving them the freedom to make their own choices and respecting their schedules, our relationships have blossomed, and our time together feels more genuine and joyful.

The Christmas of 2019 marked the first time I embraced my new outlook on holidays, and it turned out to be one of the best Christmases we've ever had. For the entire month of December, I carefully selected a Saturday when all the adults were free, and on that special day, we held a gingerbread-house-making contest while the little ones happily decorated cookies. To add to the festivities, I set up a delightful nacho bar with all the delicious toppings. The joy and laughter that filled our home on that day were indescribable, bringing warmth to even the coldest of hearts. The memory of that Christmas will forever hold a special place in my heart, reminding me of the beauty of letting go and allowing my children and their families to create their own cherished moments while still coming together to celebrate as a family.

Christmas Eve was always the highlight of my childhood Christmases, filled with cherished memories of my mom hosting a grand fondue party. The image of nine children, along with mom and dad, gathered around pots of sizzling oil, cooking and laughing together, remains etched in my heart. When I became a parent, I knew I wanted to pass on this wonderful tradition to my own children, so from the time they were little, we began our own fondue parties on Christmas Eve. The evening would culminate with a delightful chocolate fondue, the reading of the Christmas story, and the joy of receiving new pajamas for the special night. The anticipation and excitement on Christmas morning were palpable as we gathered to open the rest of the presents, savoring cinnamon rolls for breakfast, and indulging in a lavish Christmas dinner. The magic of these traditions has brought so much warmth and happiness to our home during the holiday season, creating unforgettable moments for our family.

Christmas Eve held a special place in my heart, a holiday tradition I was unwilling to compromise on even after the eye-opening family reunion at Bear Lake. I had always insisted that my children be there, and any complaints were met with an ironclad resolve. It was crucial to me, and I was not open to hearing otherwise. That year, after the transformative family counsel with my daughter Shelby, I decided to approach Christmas Eve differently. I planned the fondue dinner and a grand Christmas Day feast, just as before. However, I left the decision of when to come and receive their gifts entirely up to my children. No more guilt trips or demands; they were free to celebrate on their own terms, in their own time, meeting them where they were—always. The Christmas season of 2019 was a turning point, and since then, I have continued this newfound approach to our Christmas traditions. It has brought about wonderful outcomes and has filled our home with happiness and genuine enjoyment, making it a joyous time for my family.

As I fully embraced the lesson of meeting my grown children where they were, I realized that the same principle applied to my precious grandchildren. I wanted to include them in this newfound outlook and ensure they felt loved and cherished just as much as their parents, so I began planning special sleepovers at Grandma's house, movie nights, and any time I could have them without their parents around. Those moments of one-on-one time with them are so precious and unique. My grandchildren hold my heart in their hands, and I find myself gladly wrapped around their little fingers. I eagerly volunteer to babysit as often as possible, attending their sporting events, school programs, and Primary sacrament meeting programs. I make an effort to be present at every event they invite me to, showing them that I care and will always be there for them just as their parents are for me. Meeting them where they are has brought immeasurable joy and depth to my relationship with my grandchildren.

As I sought to strengthen my bond with my children, I stumbled upon an incredible idea shared by a friend of a friend. It dawned on me that while I had been attentive to each family unit's needs, I had overlooked the importance of giving individual attention to each child. Inspired by a couple who took their children and their spouses out to dinner monthly, I decided to adopt this practice. The children could choose the best Friday that worked for them, creating special double-date occasions.

These one-on-one outings allowed us to deepen our connection with our sons-in-law and provided a priceless opportunity to truly engage with each child. During these intimate conversations, we could learn about their well-being, desires, needs, and dreams for their family and future. The significance of these moments of individual connection became evident to me. The phrase "meet them where they are" resonated in my mind, reminding me of the importance of emulating Christ's love by genuinely meeting our children where they are, just as He so lovingly does for each of us.

Raising children in the gospel is a challenging and lifelong journey, one that never truly ends. Once a mom, always a mom. Seeing the remarkable individuals my children have grown into fills my heart with immense pride, the genuine pride that only a mother can feel when witnessing her children evolve into compassionate and

Christlike beings. Their good deeds, their selfless service to others, and the genuine love they show to their neighbors only deepen my love for each of them. With three daughters and four sons, I cherish each of these seven unique souls deeply and personally. I believe that we are given the children we are meant to raise, and they have become my greatest teachers. They exemplify unconditional love, and as I strive to meet them where they are, they, in turn, meet me where I am, creating a beautiful bond that continues to grow and strengthen over time.

The legacy I aspire to leave behind is one of meeting my grown children and grandchildren where they were. I strived to be there for them in times of need, extending invitations and opening my heart and home to them. While it would be wonderful to be the favorite or the one they wanted to be around, my ultimate hope is that they see my legacy as one of Christ's love. Just as Christ loves us unconditionally, I love my children, sons-in-law, and grandchildren with that same love. I view them through the eyes of Christ, meeting them where they are and embracing them wholeheartedly.

My greatest wish is that my approach to inviting them into my life serves as an example for them to invite their own posterity into their lives in the same Christlike manner. I believe that this legacy of love and inclusion will carry on in their lives and be passed down to future generations, becoming a cherished blessing for generations to come.

> Being a good parent requires knowing when to push and when to back off. When to help and when to let them make mistakes. Then being strong enough to watch them go.
>
> —Vidya Sury

FOLLOWING YOUR PASSIONS—THE PLACE BEYOND DREAMS

Have I not commanded you? Be Strong and Courageous.
Do not be frightened. And do not be dismayed. For
the Lord, your God is with You wherever you go.
—Joshua 1:9

Sitting by the Christmas tree with Stetsen on that delightful Arizona December afternoon, I couldn't help but feel overwhelmed with love and pride. Seeing him home on leave from the army, looking so content and joyful, brought tears of happiness to my eyes. The dark and solemn countenance that had troubled him for so many years seemed to have vanished. In its place was a bright and vibrant spirit, radiating positivity and hope. I marveled at the incredible man he had become: strong, compassionate, and driven to serve others. He was now a leader, guiding and inspiring young soldiers through his own example. My heart swelled with love for this remarkable man, my precious son.

As I sat there with Stetsen, his words struck me like a revelation. He turned to me and asked if I knew why he had chosen the military all those years ago. In that moment, I was taken aback and replied with a lighthearted joking response about playing in the dirt and shooting guns. He chuckled, but then his tone grew serious. He told me that it was because I had taught him to follow his passions, to pursue what truly fulfilled him and brought him joy. He was living his life exactly as I had taught him, following his passions and finding immense happiness in doing so.

My heart swelled with pride and love for this wise and insightful man. In that moment, I saw the impact of my teachings on his life and realized that our dreams and passions play a significant role in the legacy we leave behind. By embracing and living those dreams every day, we can inspire and impact others in ways we may never fully comprehend. How I love this boy, and how grateful I am to witness the realization of his dreams.

There is no passion to be found playing small—in settling
for a life that is less than the one you are capable of living.
—Nelson Mandela

Chapter 5

BECOMING A TEACHER

I wasn't born to "Just Teach."
I was born to inspire others.
To change people, and to never give up;
Even when faced with challenges that seem impossible.
—Anonymous

As a five-year-old surrounded by my dolls, all sitting diligently at their makeshift school desks, I proudly declared to my mom, "Someday, I am going to teach in a real classroom. I am going to teach great things to other kids like me."

My mom patted my head affectionately, a warm smile gracing her face, encouraging my dreams.

By the time I turned ten, I had transformed my playtime into an actual teaching experience. My younger brothers and sisters were now my eager students, seated at their little desks, ready to learn. I prepared worksheets for them, and with enthusiasm, I read stories, trying my best to make the lessons enjoyable. I had them sit in rows, urging them to listen attentively to me. However, managing a classroom, even a make-believe one, had its challenges.

Lance, my four-year-old brother, proved to be a particularly restless student. He refused to stay in his chair and was always fidgeting around. My older brother, unimpressed with my teaching efforts, rolled his eyes and criticized, "You are the worst teacher ever." Even though my two sisters tried their best to listen, the antics of the boys made it challenging for everyone.

Yet despite the chaos, my mom would come in from time to time, observing my teaching endeavors with a smile. Undeterred by the challenges, I reaffirmed my aspirations to her, saying, "Someday, I will have a real classroom. I will have real students sitting at desks. They will want me as their teacher." My determination was unwavering.

However, my older brother had his reservations, voicing his concerns in a frustrated tone, "You better be a nice teacher, or no one is going to like you."

I glared back at him, my determination fueled by his doubt. Growing up as the second child in a family of nine, I had plenty of opportunities to practice my teaching skills. I learned what worked and what didn't when trying to capture the attention of my young audience.

There were moments of success when my siblings would sit and listen intently, their curiosity piqued by my lessons. These moments filled me with joy and reinforced my belief that teaching was my calling. I knew deep inside that someday, I would step into a real classroom, surrounded by eager students, and make a positive impact on their lives.

As I continued to grow, my passion for teaching never wavered, and my dream to educate and inspire others burned brightly within me. Little did I know that my determination and love for teaching would shape my future and lead me down a path where I could fulfill my childhood dream of becoming a teacher, making a difference in the lives of many children just like me.

By the time I reached the age of twelve, my childhood dream of becoming a teacher remained unwavering in my heart and mind. However, the real challenge lay in finding a way to turn that dream into a reality. I knew that achieving this goal would require me to excel academically, which I was confident I could do with dedication and hard work. But there was another hurdle: the financial aspect of going to college, which seemed like a daunting concept. My dad, a passionate farmer, had struggled to sell his crops during the challenging times of the '70s and '80s.

Despite our modest means, I never felt lacking in any way. We grew our own food, and it was plentiful, providing us with a sense of abundance. Each school year, my sister and I would excitedly receive one new outfit each, and we felt fortunate to have even that. Love enveloped our family, and we learned the value of hard work from an early age. I cherished the memories of running through the fields, building forts among the trees and corn patches. It was a simple and fulfilling life, albeit one with little monetary wealth.

As I entered high school with my aspirations of becoming a teacher and making a positive impact on students' lives, the dream of going to college still burned brightly within me. I yearned to follow my passion and leave my mark on the world as an educator. However, reality hit hard during my freshman year when I came to fully understand the significant financial hurdles that stood in my way. College required a substantial amount of money, something neither I nor my parents possessed. If I was to pursue higher education, I realized that I had to find a way to achieve it on my own.

Determined to make my dreams come true, I knew I had to strive for excellent grades to be eligible for scholarships. I recognized the importance of getting a job early on to start saving for college expenses. The road ahead would be challenging, but my determination was unwavering. I held on to the belief that if I managed to get to college, everything would eventually fall into place. Little did I know that the journey to college would be more arduous than I ever imagined, testing my resolve in ways I had never dreamed possible.

With unwavering determination, I put in the hard work, striving for academic excellence and earning good grades. I took on various jobs along the way, despite the challenges of saving money. Each obstacle tested my resolve, but I remained steadfast, pushing forward with my eyes firmly fixed on the end goal. My passion for becoming a teacher served as my guiding light, propelling me forward through every difficulty and setback. No matter the hurdles, I was determined to make my dream a reality, and I knew that my perseverance and dedication would eventually lead me to the fulfilling path of becoming an educator.

The summer preceding my senior year of high school brought an unexpected upheaval as my family had to relocate. The news left me utterly devastated. I had forged strong connections and made significant progress right where we were. My high school counselors had been instrumental in helping me navigate the path to college, understanding my dreams and passions. However, the early '80s saw a crash in the farming market, leaving my dad unable to sustain his farming endeavors. Forced to make a difficult decision, he had to move us to a place where he could provide for our large family.

Looking back, I realize the tremendous challenges my parents faced in uprooting us from familiar surroundings, considering the sheer size of our family and the numerous needs to be met. It must have been an unimaginably difficult decision for them. Nevertheless, the move became inevitable, and we embarked on a new adventure, led by my mom's unwavering spirit and resourcefulness.

Starting my senior year at the new high school proved to be a challenging experience. The task of making new friends in a tight-knit community where students had grown up together since grade school felt daunting. Fortunately, I had my younger sister by my side, providing some comfort and companionship, but she quickly found her place among her peers, leaving me feeling somewhat isolated.

In the past, I had been an outgoing and involved teenager, participating in various activities at our old school. However, at this new school, I struggled to fit in and connect with others, unsure whether it was due to my senior status or my reluctance to put myself out there. The overwhelming size of the new school, twice as big as my previous one, added to my feelings of disorientation and disconnection. Having lived in our previous town since fourth grade where I knew everyone, transitioning to this new environment left me feeling lost.

Despite these challenges, I reminded myself that if I could make it through the year, college awaited me on the horizon. Holding on to this belief gave me the strength to persevere through the difficulties, working hard and giving my all to ensure I could pursue my dreams and passions in higher education.

The high school counselor at the new school proved to be a source of frustration and disappointment. In the early '80s, with an excess of schoolteachers, he seemed determined to steer me away from my dream of becoming a teacher, convinced that there was a different path better suited for me. Despite being in the top 5 percent of my class, I couldn't compete for the titles of valedictorian or salutatorian due to my limited time at the school. Missing out on those honors dashed my hopes of improving my chances for scholarships, leaving me heartbroken.

As my dreams of attending college started to fade, my counselor's lack of understanding and unwillingness to listen became increasingly apparent. He didn't take the time to know me, my passions, or what truly drove me in life. Instead, he arbitrarily enrolled me in an accounting major, aligning my course of study to that track, under the assumption that it would improve my scholarship opportunities. Despite my attempts to express my true aspirations, I found myself silenced, unable to make my voice heard. It seemed that my dreams and passions were deemed unworthy of acknowledgment and were disregarded without a second thought.

Despite the discouraging guidance from my high school counselor, I managed to secure a scholarship and Pell Grants that would cover my expenses for the first year of college. With this financial support, I was accepted into Brigham Young University, excited to embark on this new chapter in my life. While I may not have been on the education track I had dreamed of, I found solace in the fact that I was going to college and had the means to start my higher education journey. I embraced the opportunity and remained optimistic, knowing that after the first year, I could reassess my path and see where life would lead me. The uncertainty ahead didn't dampen my spirits; rather, it fueled a sense of adventure and the anticipation of discovering my true calling beyond that initial year.

My first year of college at BYU was a far cry from what I had envisioned. The enormity of the university overwhelmed me as I, a small-town farm girl, found myself amidst one of the largest campuses on the West Coast. In classes of over a thousand students, I felt lost and out of place. To make matters worse, I discovered a test-taking anxiety that had never plagued me before, leaving me struggling to perform as I had in the past.

Despite my relentless efforts, I was met with failure for the first time in my life, receiving grades below my usual As. The homesickness for the close-knit community back home, where everyone knew one another, weighed heavily on my heart. The dreams of becoming a teacher that had once burned brightly within me now seemed distant and unattainable. I began questioning whether my passion for education was merely a figment of my imagination. It felt as though I was losing a fundamental part of myself, leaving me adrift and unsure of my identity and aspirations.

During the winter of my freshman year at BYU, my parents made a significant move to Phoenix, Arizona. Despite facing challenging times and trying to find a way to provide for our family, my dad believed that Phoenix held the promise of a better life. When the spring semester at BYU ended, instead of returning to my Idaho home, I followed my heart and headed to Arizona.

As soon as I set foot in the state, I was captivated by its beauty. The warm sun, the striking red rocks, and even the desert adorned with saguaro cacti all resonated with me. It felt like home, a place where the sun never ceased to shine. Within just six months, I came to realize that my parents' move to Arizona was, in a way, meant for me. It was a place where I could envision building my own life, establishing my roots, and fulfilling my dreams. Arizona had become my home, and in that moment, I knew that I had arrived at the place where I was destined to be.

As the summer drew to a close, I found myself certain that returning to BYU was not the right path for me. My scholarship was lost, and the first year away at college had been far from enjoyable. I lacked the financial means to continue in a place where I felt utterly lost and overwhelmed. It was disheartening to feel as though I had strayed from my dreams and passions.

Despite the difficulty, I recognized that the Holy Ghost was guiding me toward a different path, one that would ultimately be better suited for me. I understood that if I heeded the Spirit's guidance, I would gather the courage to follow the Lord's plan even if its destination remained unknown to me. My heart was certain that accounting was not my calling as I loathed the business and accounting courses. The uncertainty of my college journey made me consider other options, and I eventually decided to take a job at a law office, an environment completely foreign to me. Although it was an unexpected choice, it turned out to be a wonderful job opportunity, offering both fulfillment and financial stability.

The turning point in my life came when I made the decision not to return to BYU, a decision that coincided with a fateful weekend when I met Scott at a young adult dance in Mesa. It felt like divine intervention. Meeting and eventually marrying Scott would prove to be transformative, reigniting my dreams and passions of becoming a teacher. With his unwavering support, Scott encouraged me to pursue my calling, reminding me that following our passions is an essential part of fulfilling the Lord's plan for each of us.

As we began our life together, I enrolled in the local community college, embarking once more on the path to becoming an educator. Suddenly, my life had newfound purpose. I was reclaiming the aspirations of that five-year-old girl who dreamed of changing the world one student at a time. With Scott by my side, I knew I was on the right path, and together, we embraced the journey toward making a difference in the lives of others through the power of education.

My journey to obtain my bachelor's degree in elementary education from Arizona State University was anything but easy. Life has its challenges, and mine included balancing my desire for a family with my pursuit of higher education. It took me a remarkable fifteen years to achieve my academic goal. During those years, I prioritized starting a family and raising my children, leading me to take things one step at a time. I began by enrolling in single classes at community colleges, slowly accumulating credits over time.

As I reached the point where I could apply for ASU's teaching program, I fully committed to my dream and returned to college full-time for the next two years, fully immersing myself in the coursework required to obtain my teaching degree. While it was a long and challenging road, my determination to follow my passion for teaching never wavered, and with perseverance and dedication, I finally accomplished my goal of becoming an educator.

Throughout the fifteen years it took to attain my bachelor's degree, my determination to achieve my educational goal never wavered. While others might see this journey as a lifetime, to me, every moment was cherished and filled with joy. I found immense pleasure in learning new concepts, acquiring knowledge, and broadening my horizons.

However, Scott's unwavering support played an integral role in my perseverance. He understood the significance of my education and was my biggest cheerleader, constantly encouraging me to keep pushing forward. His belief in my abilities and his constant support meant everything to me and continues to be a source of immense gratitude to this day. With Scott by my side, I felt empowered to face every challenge and obstacle that came my way, making the accomplishment of my educational dream all the more meaningful and rewarding.

Becoming a teacher has been a transformative journey filled with a deep and ever-growing love for my students. Witnessing the growth and development of children and youth as they learn has become one of the most fulfilling aspects of my life. As a mother, being a teacher feels like the perfect career as it allowed me to bring my children along with me wherever I taught. Whether they were in my classroom or nearby, I cherished the moments spent with my children, always being there for them whenever they needed me.

Embracing the role of an educator not only strengthened me as an individual but also forged a profound bond with my own kids. My dream of becoming a teacher has truly blossomed into life's passion, exceedingly even my wildest expectations and leading me to a place beyond my dreams. The joy and fulfillment I experience each day in the classroom reminds me that I am living my dream and fulfilling my purpose as an educator and a mother.

My journey as an educator didn't end with a bachelor's degree; in fact, it was just the beginning. Over the course of the following fifteen years, I continued to pursue higher education and earned two master's degrees. The culmination of my educational journey came in 2019 when I proudly received my Doctor of Education degree. From that five-year-old dreamer to the accomplished educator I am today, I have traveled a long and rewarding path.

Following my passion for teaching has taken my life beyond my wildest dreams, leading me to a place where I can truly make a difference. I now understand that when we wholeheartedly pursue our passions, we find our purpose and become individuals who inspire others to do the same. In this place beyond dreams, we discover the power to encourage others to follow their own passions, creating a ripple effect that impacts lives and fosters positive change.

Throughout my journey as an educator, I aspire to leave behind a lasting legacy that reflects my unwavering commitment to never giving up on my dreams. Being a teacher has been my true passion, and I hope that my dedication to this calling serves as an inspiration to others. I desire for my impact to extend beyond the classroom, leaving a mark on the lives of those around me, instilling in them the courage to follow their own passions, whatever they may be.

My deepest wish is that my children, both sons, and daughters, will be encouraged to pursue their dreams with the same unwavering passion and determination that has guided me. I want them to embrace their dreams and let those passions guide them to wherever they desire to go, making a genuine difference in the world by following their hearts.

My life's journey has been shaped by my unyielding pursuit of my dream to become a teacher. From the tender age of five, that dream ignited a passion within me that has never faded. It led me through the ups and downs of life, guiding me to acquire knowledge, to embrace challenges, and to find my purpose as an educator.

As I move forward, I hope that my legacy will be a testament to the power of following one's dreams and passions. Through my example, I want to inspire others, especially my children, to hold fast to their dreams and to approach life with unbridled passion. May my story serve as a reminder that we each possess the ability to make a difference in this world when we pursue our dreams with unwavering dedication and a heart full of passion.

You might be the only reason a child comes to school every day.
—Anonymous

Chapter 6

CHANGING THE WORLD ONE STUDENT AT A TIME

I was born to be a teacher.
It is who I am…My calling,
My passion, My life and
My World.

—Marla Rae Anders

I can still vividly recall the exhilaration and nerves that enveloped me on the first day of my teaching career as if it happened just yesterday: the moment I stepped into my very own classroom, assigned to educate thirty-two bright fourth graders in a Title I school—my first-choice placement. Securing a position in a remarkable district was a dream come true, and to have my first preference granted was the icing on the cake.

The school I entered was one with a low socioeconomic status, housing students who yearned for guidance and support. These were the kind of young minds who craved an environment where they felt cherished and essential. From that moment forward, I was determined to make a profound impact on their lives, to inspire them to reach beyond their potential, and to foster a sense of belonging and significance within the walls of my classroom.

65

Stepping before my eager students that day was an indescribable moment filled with a mixture of anticipation and fulfillment. The journey to becoming a teacher had been a long one, but as I stood there, I knew in my heart that I was finally prepared for this role. The effort I put into setting up my classroom had paid off as everything was in its rightful place. The ambiance was just right—not overly colorful yet warm and inviting, making it a space where my students would feel comfortable and motivated to learn. The distinct scent of the whiteboard markers and the aroma unique to books lingered in the air, etching that moment into my memory forever. It was a realization that I had found my true calling. I belonged here, guiding, and shaping young minds. Moreover, having three of my four children just down the hall added a sense of comfort, knowing they were close in case they needed me. The emotions and excitement of that first day never left me. It fueled my determination to showcase to the world what I was capable of as an educator.

The greatest exemplar of my journey to becoming a good teacher has been through emulating Christ and following His profound example. He stands as the ultimate teacher, the one whom I have modeled my home life, church service, and teaching practices after. A series on YouTube, *The Chosen*, beautifully portrays Christ's life, and in the concluding episode of season 1, a poignant scene unfolds where He gathers children at His campsite to impart wisdom. What struck me deeply was how Christ knelt to their level, addressing each child individually with tenderness, love, and kindness, teaching through His own actions and behavior.

Watching this scene, it became clear to me that building a classroom where students feel safe, loved, wanted, and valued should revolve around Christ at its core. To truly see my students as Christ saw them and to teach with a love akin to His became my driving mission. By embracing His teachings, I aspire to guide my students with compassion, empathy, and understanding, fostering an environment where they can grow not just academically but also as individuals imbued with love and respect for one another.

Teaching, second only to being a full-time mother, is undeniably one of the most challenging professions. Budget cuts have led to overcrowded classrooms, and as an educator, I witnessed students facing unprecedented obstacles I had never encountered before. Many of these young learners came to school each day on an empty stomach, seeking two meals provided during the school week. What they yearned for most was not just knowledge but also stability, structure, and above all, tender loving care.

Driven by a deep desire to effect change and give these students a voice, I made it my mission to create an environment where they felt valued, listened to, and inspired to return every day. My determination was rooted in teaching them the essential skills they needed to succeed in any path they chose to pursue in life. Throughout my years in education, I had the privilege of teaching various grade levels, from kindergarten to high school English, and I even took on administrative roles. Currently, I find fulfillment in instructing at local community colleges and serving as a student-teacher supervisor.

The diverse views within the education field have opened my eyes to the importance of making a lasting impact on students' lives. Now, more than two decades later, I can only hope that my efforts have indeed made a difference for those who needed me the most.

Throughout my extensive tenure as an educator within the public school system, my unwavering focus has always been on placing the students and their needs at the very forefront. Teaching has never been about me; it has always been about the students and their growth. Even as I transitioned into administrative roles, my dedication to the students remained steadfast.

Among the countless experiences and encounters throughout my career, there are certain stories that have left an indelible mark on my life. These are the stories that have shaped me, the ones I will carry within my heart. You see, I have always considered myself a collector of kids, for my students have become like my own children. They have transformed my life in ways beyond measure, molding me into the person I am today. Being a teacher is not just a profession; it is an integral part of my identity.

Early on in my career, I came to realize the profound significance of truly understanding my students if I wanted to create a meaningful impact within the classroom and school community.

Unraveling the reasons behind their actions and behaviors was pivotal in providing the support and guidance they required. It was during a transformative workshop called "Capturing Kids' Hearts" that I gleaned invaluable insights. This workshop emphasized the essential prerequisite of connecting with a student's heart before any effective teaching could take place. Building authentic and respectful relationships between teacher and child became the bedrock upon which meaningful learning could thrive. While maintaining necessary ground rules and boundaries, it was the power of these genuine connections that made all the difference. This became my ultimate aspiration, the realm where I could genuinely influence and change the world one student at a time.

In my pursuit of building up these precious students and fostering meaningful relationships, I soon realized that prayer played a pivotal role. It became a constant in my life as I fervently prayed for my students, seeking understanding of their unique personalities and needs. I prayed for the wisdom to guide and support them effectively, tailoring my approach to each child so they could feel assured of my unwavering advocacy. Additionally, I prayed for the comfort and trust of their parents, recognizing the significance of a strong home-school connection. Prayer also served as a source of strength and resilience, empowering me to carry out my responsibilities with dedication and excellence. Those first two years of teaching became a profound lesson in the importance of prayer, one that I carried with me into the years that followed, forever shaping my approach to education and the way I nurtured my students.

In my inaugural year of teaching, I found myself in a fourth-grade classroom situated within a Title I school, where diversity and low socioeconomic status were prominent characteristics. It quickly became evident that most of my students lacked basic necessities, with a staggering 90 percent relying on free lunches provided at the school. For many, coming to school meant more than just academic learning; it was a refuge from their challenging home lives. As their teacher, I embraced the responsibility to be the one who valued and acknowledged them, offering a listening ear and a loving heart. Creating a classroom environment where they felt seen, heard, and cherished became my utmost priority, for I understood that education extended far beyond the textbooks. It was about providing a safe haven and a place where they could truly thrive.

One morning, just before the bell was due to ring, a heart-wrenching scene unfolded in my classroom. A student came running in, her tear-streaked face and bruised body telling a tale of unspeakable pain. Her mother followed closely, and it became evident that a volatile argument had erupted at home, resulting in her being physically harmed. Seeking refuge, she had sought solace within the walls of our school, running straight into my classroom.

I watched in horror as her mother tried to reach her, attempting to inflict further harm. Without hesitation, I called for help from the office, all the while positioning myself between the two, desperate to shield the girl, my student, from any more abuse. In that moment, I felt a surge of emotions: fear, sadness, anger, and a deep sense of responsibility to protect this young soul. I did everything in my power to diffuse the situation, to offer comfort and safety to the girl.

Thankfully, her mother's rage was never directed at me, but the intensity of her anger toward her own ten-year-old daughter was haunting. The assistant principal and police arrived swiftly, and her mother was taken into custody. We reached out to the girl's grandmother, who came to collect her, but sadly, after that day, she was never seen again. I tried my best to uncover what had transpired afterward, but both the girl and her grandmother seemed to vanish. I can only hope and pray that the grandmother took her somewhere safe, away from harm. At least on that harrowing day, my classroom became a safe haven for her, and I will forever cherish the memory of being there when she needed it most.

On another troubling day, as my students filtered into the classroom, I couldn't help but notice one particular boy who appeared visibly agitated, his demeanor reflecting a combination of sadness and sleep deprivation. Engaged in a group activity, the boy's emotions escalated all of a sudden, and he began yelling incoherently, seemingly angered by his group members.

Reacting swiftly, I hurried over to the group, hoping to address the situation and calm him down. But as I approached, something unexpected happened: he impulsively grabbed one end of a nearby desk and hurled it in my direction. The desk crashed noisily, and in that instant, the weight of his actions seemed to dawn on him as tears streamed down his face uncontrollably. The commotion attracted the attention of the teacher next door, who came to our aid. I entrusted her with the other students while I took the sobbing boy outside to have a conversation in an effort to understand what he was going through and to offer support.

In that heartbreaking moment, this young boy's pain was evident in his teary eyes as he shared a harrowing story with me. He revealed that the night before, the police had been called to his home due to a violent fight between his parents. His mother was taken to the hospital by ambulance, and his father ended up in jail. Subsequently, the boy found himself at the police station, waiting until the early hours of the morning for child protective services to intervene. They brought him home to change his clothes, provided him with breakfast, and then dropped him off at school.

The fear and terror he experienced during that traumatic incident were overwhelming. He expressed concerns about where he was going to live and whether his father would come after him next. In my arms, he poured out his emotions, and we both cried together for what felt like an eternity.

Eventually, he ended up in foster care but was allowed to return to class. I kept a close watch over him at school, and though he appeared okay, it was evident that he was forever changed by the ordeal. A part of my heart remains with that boy who, in a moment of distress, threw a desk at me. The depth of his pain and the impact of his experience continue to linger, serving as a powerful reminder of the profound responsibility and compassion educators bear in supporting and protecting their students.

During my first year as an educator, a profound shift occurred in my perception of parenting and what I wished to cultivate in my own home for my children. While I had always believed my husband Scott and I were good parents, I now understood that it went beyond that. I yearned for my children to feel truly safe and cherished within our family. Applying the same skills I had acquired in college, which taught me how to create a secure environment for my students, I now employed them in my own household. I opened up clear lines of communication with my children, making sure they knew they could always confide in me. Much like how I welcomed my students into my classroom each day, I greeted my children warmly as they entered our home. When they departed for school or any other occasion, I made a point to express my love for them, a trait I had learned from my husband, Scott. The happiness and well-being of my children were paramount, and I vowed to shield them from fear and sorrow. Our family made it a steadfast goal to ensure our children felt unconditionally loved, valued, and deeply honored in every aspect of their lives.

In my very first year of teaching, these two remarkable students imparted invaluable lessons that would forever shape my approach as an educator. The boy who threw the desk taught me the importance of being slow to react and serving as his advocate. Had I rushed to call for help on that tumultuous day, I would have missed the opportunity to delve into the root of his issues and gain his trust. By refraining from immediately involving others for discipline, he eventually came to see me as a confidant.

On the other hand, the abused girl taught me the significance of fearlessly standing up for these vulnerable children in the face of danger. I learned not to shy away from stepping between her and her parents, becoming a steadfast advocate for her well-being no matter the personal cost. These profound experiences reaffirmed my commitment to always prioritize the emotional and physical safety of my students, seeking to understand their struggles and champion their rights in every circumstance.

In that unforgettable first year of teaching, there was another student who left a lasting impression on me. He was a boy who seemed to have an endless stream of words, talking nonstop. It was a challenge most teachers encounter at some point in their careers. No matter what strategies I tried, he simply wouldn't cease talking. In a bid to curb his chatter, I even placed him next to my desk, thinking my presence might deter him, but it had the opposite effect, and he chatted even more, reveling in the attention.

Realizing that a direct approach was needed, I took him aside for a one-on-one conversation and gently broached the subject of his incessant talking. The shock on his face was evident as he had assumed I enjoyed our conversations. I explained that while I cherished our interactions, he needed to grasp that there were moments during the school day when talking was appropriate and times when he needed to listen and focus on his studies. It was a delicate balance to strike, but by fostering understanding and mutual respect, we worked together to find a solution that allowed him to express himself while also honoring the learning environment for everyone else.

During that poignant encounter as I tried to establish boundaries with the talkative student, I noticed a shift in his demeanor. He withdrew, his gaze fixated on his hands, and his lips quivered with unspoken emotions. Sensing his distress, I paused and invited him to share his thoughts, eager to understand why talking was so crucial to him. Tearfully, he revealed that he was the youngest of five children, living in a small house with his aunt, uncle, and three older cousins. At home, no one took the time to listen to him; his voice went unheard, and his stories were dismissed as unimportant. However, on the first day of school, he noticed that I listened attentively to one of his tales and smiled when he finished. My classroom became the only place where he felt free to speak without being ridiculed.

This poignant interaction taught me a profound lesson: each student possesses a unique voice that deserves to be heard. Although I had set boundaries in my classroom, ensuring that students knew when to speak and when to listen, I now understood the significance of actively listening to their voices. I carried this lesson beyond the classroom, applying it at home with my own children. It became clear that a child's voice should always be cherished and respected, a powerful reminder of the transformative impact we can have as educators and parents when we offer our genuine attention and receptivity.

During the subsequent year, I found myself transferred to a different school, yet again with my children following me. This time, I was entrusted with teaching fifth grade in another Title I school. The classroom was a portable one, crammed with thirty-five students, leaving barely enough space to move. To my surprise, three boys in my class were bigger than me, presenting a unique challenge. However, I embraced the opportunity to connect with each of them individually, which taught me the immense significance of listening attentively and building meaningful relationships.

As I got to know these boys, I realized that being their advocate was more crucial than ever. On three separate occasions that year, life presented me with lessons that reaffirmed the importance of these values. The impact of those experiences stayed with me then and continues to shape my approach as an educator even now. The profound lessons learned from those boys have become an integral part of my teaching philosophy and a constant reminder of the transformative power of genuine connections and advocacy in the lives of our students.

The memory of the first boy I encountered during my teaching career remains etched in my mind, leaving an indelible impact that would extend far beyond that particular school year. He was a Hispanic student, heavyset, and towering over me by two to three inches. Around two months into the school year, a concerning pattern emerged: he began getting kicked off the bus before it even left the school premises, and the bus drivers would bring him to me. Together, we would then walk to the principal's office, attempting to find someone who could come and pick him up. Despite my persistent inquiries, he remained tight-lipped, providing no explanation for his disruptive behavior.

Nevertheless, I made it my mission to check on him and his well-being for years to come, seeking to understand the underlying reasons behind his actions and offering support in any way possible. That boy's enigmatic struggles taught me the profound responsibility we carry as educators to be there for our students not just academically but also emotionally and personally, ensuring they know they are cared for and valued in every aspect of their lives.

After three days of persistent questioning, the truth finally emerged from the boy's tearful eyes as he bravely revealed his painful reality. He expressed a desperate desire to go home with me, knowing that I had other children and had often spoken about them in class. In a heart-wrenching disclosure, he shocked me by admitting that his mother was subjecting him to frequent physical abuse, leaving him terrified to return home.

As much as I wished I could take him in, I knew it was not within my power, and it was not permitted. Together, we walked in silence to the principal's office, where we laid bare the troubling situation. We reached out to child protective services, initiating an investigation. Unfortunately, because of his Hispanic origin and darker skin, the bruises he bore were difficult to see, and his mother denied the allegations. Heartbreakingly, he remained in that environment. Despite the uphill battle, he continued to come to school, and I did my utmost to care for him the best way I knew how. Through it all, he maintained an unyielding smile that had the power to soften anyone's heart, a beacon of resilience that spoke volumes about his courage and strength.

It breaks my heart to admit that by the time he reached the age of seventeen, he found himself in prison, a tragic consequence of fighting back against the abuse he endured at home. I firmly believe that he would never have resorted to violence unless he had reached a breaking point, unable to endure the pain any longer. To my dismay, it was his own mother who turned him in, accusing him of being the abuser instead. I cannot shake the feeling in my heart that he was unfairly judged, and the circumstances pushed him to this drastic measure as a means of self-preservation.

This devastating experience only solidified my commitment to watch out for these vulnerable children, to be their advocate and protector. Over the years, these students became like my own children, and with each passing grade level, they took a piece of my heart with them, etching a lasting impact on my life and reaffirming the significance of nurturing a safe and caring environment for all students.

The second boy I encountered that year came to me a few months into the school term. He was a heavyset white eleven-year-old, towering over me by a good six inches, and despite his young age, he appeared much older, burdened with the weight of his circumstances. Every day, without fail, he would fall into a deep, snoring sleep in my class, regardless of the subject or activity at hand.

Concerned for him, I sat him down one day and asked why he slept so much in my classroom. He bravely shared his heartbreaking story. His mother had left, taking the money they had for drugs, leaving him and his dad to live in a weekly paid hotel. I knew the hotel he spoke of, and it was no place for an eleven-year-old. His dad had lost his job but managed to find a new one, though he had to work nights, leaving the boy alone in the hotel.

He lived in constant terror, unable to sleep at night, fearing that the gunshots he heard were meant for him and that the people yelling and screaming outside his door were coming to harm him. He was a child plagued with fear, seeking solace in my classroom, the only place he felt safe and at peace. This heart-wrenching experience opened my eyes to the profound impact a safe and nurturing environment can have on a child's well-being and development, inspiring me to create a classroom where every student feels cared for and protected.

Through the collective efforts of the principal and myself, we were able to extend a helping hand to the father and son, who were facing such dire circumstances. Utilizing the district's available resources and programs, we swiftly intervened, and soon enough, the boy began arriving at school well rested and eager to learn. After the dust had settled, he approached me a few weeks later, pulling me aside to express his gratitude. He acknowledged that I wasn't his biological mother, but to him, I had become just that: his mom. My heart swelled with emotion once more as I realized the profound impact our support had on him.

As he moved forward, he carried with him a piece of my heart, and years later, I would receive news that he had become a teacher himself. He had chosen to give back, inspired to pass on the lessons and love I had bestowed upon him, completing a heartwarming cycle of care and compassion that touched my life in the most meaningful way.

The third young boy I had the privilege of teaching was a true gem. He came from a wonderful family with a loving home life and was an all-around good-hearted child. However, he faced a single challenge in life: English proficiency. Determined to help him overcome this hurdle, I dedicated countless hours to tutoring him, providing guidance on how to apply his English skills effectively in other subject areas. His parents were incredibly supportive, coming to school after hours to converse with me in English, reinforcing what their son was learning in the classroom. Witnessing not only my student but his entire family become more fluent in English was a truly rewarding experience.

Another heavyset Hispanic boy towering over me by three inches, he and the two other boys from previous experiences would spend their recesses walking around with me while I was on duty, forgoing playtime with others. They preferred engaging in conversations with me, eager to discuss what they had learned. The bond we shared and the transformation I witnessed in their lives paralleled the profound impact they had on mine, creating a remarkable interplay of growth and inspiration for us all.

On a warm spring afternoon, in a rare move, I had the classroom door open to the outside, inviting the pleasant weather and sunshine into our learning space. As we delved into a story, reading it aloud and discussing characters and their actions, a looming shadow disrupted our peaceful atmosphere. Turning to the door, I saw a towering man, standing at close to six feet five inches with a stocky build, unmistakably Native American. He was approaching me rapidly, pointing his finger and yelling.

Initially, shock paralyzed me, and I struggled to comprehend his words. However, my first instinct was to protect my students, so I mustered the courage to step closer to him as he advanced into the center of the room. The thirty-five students in the class remained silent, their eyes wide with apprehension. Gradually, I managed to calm the man down and understand the reason for his agitation: his grandson, who was in my class, had refused to come into the school and was waiting in the car. He implored me to go to the parking lot and bring his grandson into class.

The man's imposing figure continued to approach, towering over my petite five-foot frame, while my heart raced with fear. In a desperate attempt to maintain some distance, I instinctively put up my hands and asked him to stop. Unknowingly, as I took a slight step back, I inadvertently backed into the three boys who had always been there for me, my protectors. Their reassuring presence gave me strength, and when the man saw them standing behind me, their arms folded, they spoke those words that would resonate deeply within me: "We got you, Mrs. West." Surprisingly, those simple words halted the man's advance.

Just then, a neighboring teacher, drawn by the commotion, arrived at my classroom. Together, we managed to calm the agitated grandfather and promptly informed the principal of the situation. As he left, the students sat there, shell-shocked, still in silence, except for my three boys, my protectors, who remained steadfastly behind me like sentinels. Their unwavering support and courage in that moment were nothing short of amazing, reminding me of the incredible impact we can have on each other's lives, creating a bond that transcends age and roles.

Throughout my teaching journey, I've been blessed with an abundance of heartwarming memories and countless students who have left indelible footprints on my soul. They have taught me invaluable lessons, not only on how to grow as a teacher but also as a better mother. At the end of each day, I would return home to my supportive husband Scott and our children, sharing with them the stories of my students and the wonders we explored in the classroom.

As I honed my ability to understand and cater to each student's unique learning style, I also discovered how to guide and support my own children in becoming better students. These shared experiences have enriched my life in immeasurable ways, shaping me into a more empathetic, compassionate, and skilled educator and mother. My students have gifted me with moments of joy, growth, and discovery, and I cherish each and every one of them, for they have left an everlasting mark on my heart and soul.

There are stories from my teaching career that still haunt me to this day. One such memory involves a little kindergarten student who arrived at school with chunks of her hair brutally cut off so close to the scalp that it was bleeding. As a mandatory reporter, I immediately took action and reported the disturbing incident to our school's resource officer.

A few days later, the police visited the little girl's home, only to discover her and her three sisters standing in holes outside, holes that had been dug by their mother's boyfriend as a cruel form of punishment. The girls were made to stand in those holes, sprayed with water while clad only in their underwear. The eldest girl was fourteen, and the youngest was just five years old. The consequences of reporting such abuse were severe, as the mother later called me, accusing me of taking away her welfare money when the four girls were removed from her home.

This was not the first time nor the last time I had to contact child protective services to protect my students from harm. Regrettably, such actions often led to receiving death threats for simply doing what was right for the children under my care. Despite the distressing experiences, I remained committed to advocating for the well-being of my students as every child deserves to be safe, loved, and cherished.

As I transitioned into an administrative role at the district level, my commitment to prioritizing students' needs remained unwavering. I spearheaded the creation of programs aimed at enhancing children's reading and math development, recognizing the pivotal role these skills play in their overall academic journey.

Furthermore, I implemented comprehensive classroom-management programs and provided training to teachers, striving to foster an environment where students felt safe, valued, and respected within the school walls. Understanding the significance of effective communication between home and school, I advocated for every teacher to make positive phone calls to parents, establishing a strong bond between families and the school community.

These efforts culminated in some of the most successful years in education for me as I served as the curriculum and federal programs director. Witnessing student achievement reaching new heights, observing students' newfound confidence in coming to school, and witnessing an increase in teacher morale affirmed that I was indeed making a positive difference in the lives of those I served. These rewarding moments fueled my passion for educational leadership, encouraging me to continue advocating for the well-being and success of all students under my care.

As the curriculum and federal programs director, a crucial aspect of my role was overseeing the well-being of homeless students within the district. Although we didn't have a large number of homeless students, I remained committed to ensuring they received the care and support they deserved. I vividly recall one bitterly cold winter when five families were living out of their cars, struggling to cope with the harsh conditions.

Determined to help, I would visit these families once a week, driving to the locations where they were known to park at night. My visits served as a way to check on their well-being, ensuring they had enough gas to keep their cars warm and enough food to sustain themselves. In an effort to battle the cold, I provided them with blankets to offer some relief. My commitment to these families continued throughout my entire tenure as the director as I firmly believed that every child, regardless of their circumstances, deserved a chance to thrive and succeed in school and in life.

During the last two years of my time in K–12 education, before transitioning to teaching in colleges, I served as a high school assistant principal. The first year was truly rewarding as I had the opportunity to work under a kind and compassionate principal, allowing me to focus on meeting the needs of our students and making a positive impact. However, the second year proved to be challenging as a new principal took over who displayed little kindness and seemed to lack a genuine fondness for children. I struggled to understand her motivations for being in the educational field.

Our conflicting views became apparent in many areas, with discipline of the students being the most contentious. She insisted on removing "problematic" students from the school and advocated for issuing suspensions of up to nine days, regardless of the offense. This approach did not align with my values as I firmly believed that such lengthy suspensions could leave students unsupervised at home, which could be detrimental to their well-being and development.

My dedication to fostering a supportive and inclusive learning environment clashed with her disciplinary approach, leading to a difficult and emotionally taxing year. Despite the challenges, I remained steadfast in my commitment to advocating for the best interests of our students, ensuring their safety, growth, and success were at the forefront of my decisions and actions.

Navigating the delicate balance between following expectations and staying true to my beliefs in discipline became a challenge that weighed heavily on me. While I attempted to fulfill my role, the disconnect between the punitive approach my new principal advocated and my belief in supporting students to keep them in school persisted. By December, I made a personal commitment to find a middle ground, seeking ways to help these troubled students without being insubordinate. I knew in my heart that they needed positive role models and compassionate support to thrive.

Determined to make a difference, I embarked on a mission to track down about eight students whom I consistently saw in my office, struggling academically and behaviorally. Throughout the day, during passing times, lunch breaks, and before or after school in the courtyard, I would approach them, hoping to establish connections and understand their challenges better. It became clear that my daily footsteps were a testament to my dedication to reaching out and offering a helping hand to the students who were overlooked and dismissed by others. I was determined to be their advocate, providing the support and guidance they so desperately needed to find success in the classroom and beyond.

During that year, one of the Light the World tasks encouraged us to seek out those who needed our support. With this task in mind, I felt a deep sense of responsibility toward the eight troubled students I had been concerned about. I was determined to connect with each of them in a meaningful way within the day's time frame. My commitment was unwavering, and I began early that morning by carefully studying each student's schedule, making a detailed plan of when and where I would approach them. However, navigating the complexities of a high school schedule proved to be challenging, and I soon realized that schedules rarely unfolded as planned.

Nevertheless, I remained steadfast in my determination to reach out to these students, even if it meant adapting my approach and seizing unexpected opportunities to connect with them. With my heart set on making a positive impact on their lives, I pressed on, ready to adapt and be there for them in whatever way I could.

The morning proved to be a series of unfortunate events, with unexpected disruptions and challenges hindering my efforts to reach out to the students who needed me. Fire drills, students caught smoking, and technical difficulties were just a few of the obstacles that threw my carefully planned schedule into disarray. By lunchtime, I had only managed to connect with one student, leaving seven more to go.

Undeterred, I remained determined to accomplish my goal and meet these students where they were, relying on the guidance of the Spirit to let me know if they were doing well. As I entered the bathroom, I locked the door and began to pray, seeking strength to navigate the rest of the day and hoping for the school's issues to subside. Above all, my most fervent prayer was that I would find a way to reach each of these students by the end of the day and provide them with the support and understanding they needed in that moment. My heart was resolute, and I knew that if I kept my faith, I could make a difference in their lives, even if only for that one December day.

Undeterred by the challenges of the morning, I approached the task with renewed determination and commitment. Instead of waiting for passing times between classes, I decided to take a more direct approach by pulling students from their classes to speak with them. I understood that my actions might not be well received by the principal, so I carefully planned my interactions, ensuring that they aligned with her schedule to avoid any potential interference.

Throughout the afternoon, I felt an undeniable pull to complete the Light the World task, as if something greater than myself was guiding me. I knew deep down that I had to keep trying and pushing forward to achieve this goal for the sake of those eight students who needed my support. It was not about me; it was about making a difference in their lives, and that purpose drove me to continue even in the face of obstacles and potential opposition.

On that special December day, I achieved my mission of reaching all eight students who needed me. Throughout the day, I felt a profound presence of Christ with me, guiding and supporting me in connecting with each of these individuals. It was as if He had orchestrated their presence in my path, leading me to light their world that day.

One particular moment stood out to me: when I approached a tall basketball player who seemed puzzled as to why I had sought him out. As we spoke, I could see his initial panic turn to shock when he realized that I, a mere five-foot-tall individual, cared enough to take the time to talk to him. This boy, often in trouble and feeling unsupported, was genuinely surprised that someone was there for him. From that moment onward, he knew he had someone in his corner, someone who would drop everything to check on him, make sure he was okay, and ensure he had everything he needed. My heart swelled with gratitude and fulfillment, knowing that by simply reaching out and offering a listening ear, I had made a lasting impact on his life.

As I continue my journey as an educator at the college level, I am grateful that my approach to teaching and building relationships with students remains unchanged. Whether my students are older than me or just beginning their educational journey, they all become my kids. Throughout my years in education, I have been incredibly blessed to teach a diverse range of students, each with unique backgrounds, learning levels, and cultural experiences. These varied encounters have enriched my life beyond measure, defying any description. From that little five-year-old girl's dream of becoming a teacher, my passion has driven me to soar and leave a meaningful mark on the world of education. My heart is filled with gratitude as I continue to fulfill that dream by making a difference in the lives of those I have the privilege to teach and guide.

The legacy I hope to leave for my posterity is one of goodness and compassion, inspiring them to make a positive impact on the world one person at a time. I wish for them to recognize that their dreams and passions hold the potential to be powerful forces for good, leading them to utilize their God-given talents to create meaningful change. My ultimate hope is that their lives are driven by their passions, taking them to places beyond their wildest dreams, where they can truly make a difference and spread love and kindness to those around them. I hope they will embrace the teachings of Christ both in their actions and their hearts, embracing a life of service, empathy, and love for all humanity.

With a heart full of compassion and determination, I have been able to make a lasting impact on the lives of countless students. From the early years of teaching in a Title I school to the college level, I have strived to exemplify the importance of building strong relationships, understanding each student's unique needs, and valuing the power of education to transform lives.

The experiences I shared here have highlighted the challenges and joys of teaching, reminding us of the deep connections that can be formed between educators and their students. My commitment to making a positive difference in the lives of others and leaving a legacy of love and service for future generations is a testament to the power of teaching as a truly noble and transformative profession.

You must capture a kid's heart.
To get to his head.
If that is not where you start,
Please do another job instead.
Kids must know you
to be true.
And the key to that is without a doubt…YOU!
—Dr. George Luck

Part 3

Staying the Course, No Matter What

> Just stay the course,
> And do what it is that you do.
> And grow while you are doing it.
> Eventually, it will either come full circle,
> Or at least you will go to bed at night happy.
>
> —Jon Bon Jovi

In the dim confines of Liberty Jail, Joseph Smith found himself in dire straits, his body shivering with cold, stomach gnawing with hunger, and his only bed a dirty, uncomfortable floor. Above him, crude men taunted and jeered, adding to his torment.

Amidst this desolation, the prophet turned to his Heavenly Father, seeking solace and pouring out his heart in fervent prayer but feeling as though his pleas went unanswered. Yet in that darkness, a divine response pierced through the silence:

> My son, peace be unto thy soul: thine adversity and thine afflictions shall be but a small moment; And then, if thou endure it well, God shall exalt thee on high; thou shalt triumph over all thy foes. (Doctrine and Covenants 121:7–8)

Foes—the word echoed in his mind, an intriguing term that extended beyond physical adversaries to include unseen and internal battles. Joseph contemplated how in life, trials often manifest in the form of tangible opponents or physical challenges, but just as frequently, they lurk within the depths of our minds, unseen foes that wage mental anguish. These internal battles are not easily won, demanding unwavering endurance and courage.

In this moment of profound revelation, Joseph Smith learned that adversities and foes, both seen and unseen, were not insurmountable obstacles but opportunities for growth and divine refinement. Like the prophet, we all face struggles that test our spirits, and sometimes, the greatest battles are fought within. Yet as we seek divine aid and persevere through these trials with faith and resilience, we can find strength, overcome adversity, and ultimately triumph over the foes that seek to defeat us.

My motto in life has become, "Everything that happens to me is for my good and the betterment of myself." Through the lens of this belief, I have come to understand that every trial and struggle I encounter in life serves a purpose in shaping who I am meant to be. These experiences have been instrumental in preparing me to fulfill my roles as a parent, a friend, a colleague, and a ministering sister. I have learned that life's journey is not meant to be easy. Challenges are inevitable, but they are also invaluable opportunities for growth.

Embracing this perspective, I aim to leave behind a meaningful legacy, one that reflects how I faced each day with courage, resilience, and unwavering determination to become the best version of myself.

Chapter 7

TRIALS, ANXIETY, DEPRESSION

Every trial and experience you have passed
through is necessary for your salvation.
—Brigham Young

On that somber October night, the world around me slumbers, but I am engulfed in an overwhelming darkness that seems unbearable. The pain, both physical and emotional, weighs heavily on my weary soul, and all I yearn for is respite. It feels as though I can no longer glimpse the light amidst the suffocating shadows. The pills laid out on the kitchen table beckon to me, a desperate temptation to bring an end to this ceaseless suffering. As I stare at the glass of water beside them, my heart wrestles with conflicting emotions, desperately seeking the courage to take that step—to find an escape from it all, to ease the burden, and to dissipate the fog of despair. In this desolate moment, I grapple with the profound desire to see the dawn of hope once more.

To this very day, I cannot ascertain the exact duration I sat there, locked in a battle of emotions and thoughts, contemplating an end I wasn't sure I truly wanted. The conflicting voices waged war within me, one urging me not to take the pills, while the other enticingly whispered to give in and put an end to it all. As the faces of my precious children appeared in my mind, I tried to push them away, feeling guilt wash over me. Then unexpectedly, the faces of the

Young Women I ministered to came into view, and a fleeting but poignant thought emerged: what would they think if I succumbed to this darkness?

Before I knew it, I found myself propelled into my bedroom, seeking solace from Scott, yearning for his assistance in accomplishing this desperate task I craved at that moment. I will never forget the shock in his eyes, the way he pulled me close, crying with me, unsure of what to do. Eventually, that year, I sought and received the help I needed, but it took a medical emergency—having to undergo gallbladder surgery—to find someone who could truly aid me in overcoming the overwhelming darkness that had consumed me.

Trials are an inevitable part of our earthly journey, foreknown in the pre-earth life as a crucial aspect of the divine plan. It was there, in the presence of our loving Heavenly Father and Jesus Christ, that we willingly embraced this mortal experience as a means to find our way back to them. Each of us treads a unique path beset with its own set of challenges and struggles. But amidst our individual trials, we must remember that everyone, without exception, faces their own battles. These trials are not meant to break us but to mold us, to teach us valuable lessons and strengthen our character.

In our darkest moments, it may be difficult to fathom the purpose of such trials, but as time unfolds, we come to realize that the wisdom gained from these experiences takes time to fully blossom. It is the very essence of trials that propels us to continuously learn, to grow, and to find solace in following the path that the Lord has laid out for us. Through the lens of faith, we find purpose in our trials and seek to support and uplift others as they navigate through their own challenges, fostering a greater sense of compassion and unity among all of God's children.

In 2013, Elder Jeffery R. Holland delivered a powerful and poignant general conference talk titled "Like a Broken Vessel," which resonated deeply with many, especially those grappling with depression and emotional challenges. Elder Holland emphasized the significance of finding peace and understanding amidst these struggles while staying true to the Lord's plan for our lives.

Reflecting on the events that led up to that dark October night, I now recognize the mistakes I had made in the years preceding it, mistakes that involved suppressing and concealing my pain, wearing a mask of happiness to hide my internal turmoil from those around me. Each day was a battle, and I tried my best to cope as I navigated through the aftermath of my son Stetsen's devastating accident, dealing with the weight of his traumatic brain injury.

Amidst the difficulties, I couldn't shake the feeling that I had failed as a mother, that I had somehow not adequately prepared him spiritually before the accident, leading to his estrangement from the faith. This self-doubt consumed me, adding to the burden of guilt and inadequacy that I felt, convinced that I was perpetually falling short as a parent and letting down my son when he needed me the most.

I made desperate attempts to seek help, feeling the weight of my struggles bearing down on me. My first stop was my ob-gyn, hoping he could offer some relief or connect me with someone to talk to, but instead, he dismissed my pain, attributing it solely to my imagination. Turning to the church services, I found they weren't accepting new patients, and even my primary care physician claimed to have no record of me, refusing to take on any more patients.

My husband, Scott, encouraged me to persist, but it felt like a futile endeavor. No one seemed willing to extend a helping hand. The growing sense that maybe it was all in my head haunted me, leaving me to confront my ordeal in silence. In doing so, I merely pushed it aside, avoiding true confrontation and resolution of my suffering.

In December, the pain in my abdomen escalated to the point where I found myself in the emergency room, diagnosed with a severe case of gallbladder issues. When asked about my primary care physician, I was forced to admit that I either didn't have one or was no longer listed as their patient.

It was then that a compassionate and perceptive nurse took charge, sensing the urgency of the situation. Despite my lack of proper documentation, she took the initiative to contact my doctor and requested her to come and attend to me. It was as if she was divinely inspired, guided by a still small voice within her, leading her to reach out to my physician. Perhaps she saw a hint of desperation in my eyes, or maybe the Spirit whispered to her that I needed help beyond just the physical ailment. This nurse's act of kindness and intuition would prove to be a turning point, leading me toward the assistance I had been seeking for so long.

Finally, the help I had been desperately seeking found its way to me through an unexpected surgery in December. It was divine intervention. The nurse's path crossed with mine precisely when I needed it most. I've witnessed divine intervention countless times in my life, a testament to God's boundless grace that aids us when we've done all we can on our own. With this fortuitous encounter, I was able to open up to a professional about the challenges I was facing, an essential step toward healing.

However, life's demands and distractions once again interfered, causing me to prematurely discontinue the much-needed therapy, an unfortunate decision that I later came to regret. Scott, my husband, urged me to persist with therapy, but stubbornness or exhaustion prevented me from following through. I now recognize that I should not have halted the therapy until I was genuinely prepared to relinquish the help it provided. It was yet another hard-learned lesson on my journey with depression and anxiety, teaching me the value of perseverance and the significance of availing oneself of the support and resources available for our well-being.

Our greatest trial in life centered around our beloved son Stetsen, the wayward child, the one who wandered like the prodigal son in the Scriptures. In the aftermath of his accident, a year passed, and Stetsen began to drift away from our sight, rekindling connections with old acquaintances who were not the best influence. He enlisted in the marines but remained part-time, and my worries for him consumed me. Stetsen became my struggle, my constant concern.

Over the ensuing years, I faced hurtful comments from colleagues and neighbors who blamed me for his straying, implying that my shortcomings as a mother were to blame. My own perceptions, fueled by these words, led me to believe that I would never regain my son. The hurtful words of others, including a Relief Society president who questioned my worthiness for a job held by a man and a priesthood leader who felt high-paying jobs should go to men, further contributed to my self-doubt. Tragically, I allowed their opinions to shape my perception of myself as a mother and as a woman, relentlessly berating myself for my mistakes and shortcomings.

It took me years to overcome the hurtful words and judgments people directed at me for being a working mom. In hindsight, I realized that I had the best job in the world: being a mother. Whether I was at work or not, my children were always close by, and I could be with them at a moment's notice, especially since I worked in the schools they attended. The proximity allowed me to attend to them swiftly whenever they needed me, such as when they got injured or participated in school assemblies. My office was just a short walk away from their schools, making it possible to balance both roles effectively. My career as a teacher and school administrator played a significant role in shaping who I am today, but a substantial part of my identity will always revolve around being a devoted and loving mother to my children.

As the challenges with Stetsen resurfaced, I unintentionally shut down and ceased seeking help from my doctor. I suppressed my struggles with depression and anxiety, refusing to discuss the hurtful comments and beliefs others had imposed on me, and tragically, I allowed myself to believe those hurtful words. In doing so, I buried my pain deep within, convinced that I could handle it alone.

However, this suppression would only lead to a dangerous buildup of emotions, and after years of bottling it up, the pressure exploded. It was a tumultuous eruption that nearly brought me to the brink once again, mirroring the depths of despair experienced on that dark October night. The consequences of internalizing my pain were severe, emphasizing the critical importance of acknowledging and addressing mental health challenges openly and proactively to prevent them from resurfacing in harmful ways.

Depression, as defined, is a debilitating medical illness that casts a pervasive shadow over a person's emotions, thoughts, and actions. For me, it enveloped my entire being, shrouding my mind in a dense fog and causing physical pain throughout my body. I felt an overwhelming sense of self-loathing, believing that I looked terrible all the time, leading me to assume that my husband, Scott, would not want to be with me either. My sleep was disturbed, and anger became a frequent companion. The once-vibrant connection to the Spirit seemed severed, leaving me numb to any emotional experience. Describing depression proves challenging as it manifests differently in each person. In my case, it felt like a dark, cold, and isolated place, where my cries for help fell on deaf ears, and a sense of emptiness prevailed. Even my eternal companion, Scott—the love of my life—couldn't reach me in this desolate realm, leaving me feeling utterly alone.

Then there is anxiety. Anxiety, often regarded as a normal and even healthy human emotion, is something that every person encounters at some point in life. While I may have reservations about accepting it as entirely normal, experts assert its commonality, and I must respect their perspective.

However, it is when anxiety escalates to disproportionate levels that it becomes a cause for concern. This heightened form of anxiety induces excessive nervousness, fear, apprehension, and worry, which I would later come to intimately understand in my own life. The burden of severe anxiety can be overwhelming, affecting various aspects of daily living and highlighting the importance of addressing mental health challenges to lead a fulfilling and balanced life.

For three long years, I endured the harrowing experience of being stalked, and through it all, I emerged as a survivor. The severe anxiety and fear that this ordeal brought into my life were tremendous obstacles to overcome. It was a male colleague, with whom I shared offices at the school district, whose actions haunted me. Merely two doors down from my own workspace, we had both applied for the same job, but it was I who secured the position. However, he perceived a sense of entitlement, believing he deserved the job instead, and from there, his determination to undermine me and seize the opportunity for himself began to unfold. The struggle to protect my job and my sense of security took an immense toll, yet my resilience and strength ultimately prevailed, making me a survivor of an ordeal that tested the depths of my emotional and mental fortitude.

The torment of stalking commenced with his intrusive actions, disrupting my meetings held in my office or the nearby conference room. Repeatedly, he would stroll past my door, casting curious glances inside to monitor my activities. To my astonishment, I counted an astounding eighty-five times he walked by my office in a single day. His unsettling behavior escalated further as he strategically positioned himself at the lunch table, ensuring a clear view of my office. If I dared to shut my door for privacy, he would brazenly open it, even resorting to using a doorstop to keep it perpetually ajar. His secretary also became complicit in his disturbing actions, meticulously recording my comings and goings from the building, documenting my meetings, and eavesdropping on my phone conversations. The relentless surveillance created an atmosphere of constant unease, where my sense of safety and privacy eroded, and my work environment turned into a place of anxiety and fear.

As the third year of stalking drew to a close, his behavior escalated into audacious and alarming acts. He went to extreme lengths, following me to meetings at schools, shamelessly inserting himself into gatherings with teachers despite having no relevance to the proceedings. His unwelcome presence extended beyond the school premises, tracking my movements even outside the district, to lunch outings, and even meetings with the superintendent. Everywhere I turned, his car seemed to follow, a constant reminder of his intrusive watchfulness.

The stalking even invaded my sacred space, as he showed up uninvited at church one Sunday, ostensibly checking if I was actively attending my meetings. The boundary between public and private life blurred, and I became increasingly fearful as I noticed his car passing my house at night. The terror of the unknown consumed me. Why was he there? What if he ventured inside my home when no one else was around?

The perpetual anxiety and fear were suffocating. I lived in constant apprehension of potential harm, unsure of his mental state and when he might lash out. This unrelenting dread compelled me to acknowledge that something had to change, and I could no longer endure this torment in silence.

Throughout this harrowing period, I concealed the torment of the stalking from my husband, Scott, for many years. It was difficult to accept that such a situation could happen to me, as I prided myself on being independent and strong-willed. In denial, I struggled to acknowledge that I had allowed this to occur, grappling with the idea that I might have unintentionally encouraged his behavior. Feeling responsible for his actions, I chose to remain silent, hoping and praying that the torment would dissipate or cease altogether.

It wasn't until years later, when I sought therapy, that I finally recognized the gravity of what I had experienced, the therapist aptly labeling it as *stalking*. Her guidance and support empowered me to break my silence and reveal the dark truth of that period to Scott. Without her intervention, I might have never found the courage to share the painful truth with my husband, but her assistance enabled me to face the reality of my past and the healing process together.

Over those three years, I had made multiple attempts to seek help from my superintendent. The secretary of the colleague involved had carelessly left her logs about me stacked on her desk, which allowed me to discover her actions and make copies of those logs for my superintendent. However, he seemed dismissive of the situation, believing that the man would not cause me any harm, even as the stalking escalated to the point of him driving by my house, indicating a sinister shift in his intentions. The fear became unbearable, and it was clear that this was no longer about him wanting my job. It had taken an evil turn.

Frustration and desperation reached a breaking point, and I confronted my superintendent, imploring him to take action, or else I would resign. Even then, he failed to grasp the seriousness of the situation. Unable to contain my emotions, I broke down in tears, a rarity for me as I despised crying in front of others. Consumed by anger and disappointment at his inaction, I made a difficult decision: I quit. Storming back to my office, I began packing up my belongings, determined to take matters into my own hands and protect myself from this relentless torment.

Upon witnessing my distress, the superintendent visited my office and offered comfort and reassurance. He recognized the severity of my fear and the urgent need for help. As a measure to address the situation, the colleague responsible was relocated to a different building, but he was not terminated from his position, which might have been beyond the superintendent's authority. However, even with this action, I don't believe the stalking truly ceased until I moved away from the small town we lived in, where the colleague's family held significant influence.

Fearing that no one in the community would believe that he had stalked me, I hesitated to press charges, a decision I now regret. I wish I had taken legal action, if only to bring attention to what was happening and hold him accountable for his actions. Sharing my experience openly might have helped others recognize the seriousness of stalking and the necessity for vigilance in addressing such harmful behaviors.

The shame and embarrassment of what I had endured led me to once again bury a situation that demanded examination and discussion. I couldn't bring myself to confide in Scott about the stalking, overwhelmed by feelings of humiliation and self-blame. Doubts plagued my mind: had I inadvertently given the man signals that I welcomed his advances? Was the job I held so valuable to him that he resorted to such behavior?

For an extended period, I questioned every aspect of my actions, mercilessly berating myself for allowing this torment to unfold, permitting depression and anxiety to consume me once more. I maintained a facade of happiness, concealing the inner turmoil from others, terrified of being seen as a victim. But this only compounded the issue, enabling the fear to intensify and take root, festering within me. The weight of this unaddressed trauma darkened my countenance and eroded my optimism about education, my aspirations for my family, students, teachers, and fellow church members. By evading the issues, I inadvertently allowed the situation to worsen, and it became imperative for me to confront these challenges in order to find healing and reclaim my life.

Over the course of several years, our lives continued to be marked by struggles. Our challenges with Stetsen persisted, and I battled my depression and anxiety in silence, deepening the distance between Scott and me as the weight of our trials wore us down. We experienced numerous relocations, each one adding to the uncertainty we faced. Scott's business, once thriving, took a hit as the economy faltered, leading to changes in his employment.

Amidst these difficulties, we also mourned the loss of my father-in-law, a constant presence in our lives, whom I had grown to respect and love almost as much as my own dad. His passing left yet another hole in our already-fractured hearts and souls, further compounding the pain we carried. The cumulative effect of these challenges tested our resilience and strained our spirits, leaving us in search of solace and healing in the midst of life's trials.

In my second year as an assistant high school principal, my world came crashing down under the oppressive leadership of the principal I worked for, a tyrant and a toxic individual. No matter what I did, nothing seemed to satisfy her; my efforts were always deemed inadequate. Late-night calls berated me, telling me I was unworthy and terrible at my job. Rather than focusing on helping students, she pushed for a punitive approach, urging me to remove problematic students from the school by suspending them repeatedly. Moreover, she criticized me for supporting teachers, asserting that my role was not to assist them in improving but to give poor evaluation scores to those she deemed inadequate.

These conflicting expectations clashed with my values, eroding my dreams and passions, and causing me to lose sight of the students and teachers I was meant to lead. I felt myself drifting from the path set by the Lord, a path that had once provided me with purpose and direction. Overwhelmed and discouraged, I found myself slipping further from the path, and despite my prior determination, the difficulties of my situation had me teetering on the brink of giving up entirely.

The constant surveillance continued, this time orchestrated by another assistant principal who diligently documented every perceived mistake I made, all under the direction of the toxic principal. Though not as intense as before, the watchful eyes left me feeling utterly paranoid about my every action and interaction. The weight of these relentless observations left me on edge, constantly questioning myself and second-guessing my decisions. The school became a suffocating environment, and I felt myself fracturing from within.

Despite the turmoil, I felt trapped, unsure of how to escape the oppressive atmosphere. My lifelong dream of being an educator, of changing the world one student at a time, seemed to fade before my very eyes. The passion I once had for education slipped away at an alarming rate, leaving me disheartened and questioning my purpose. The joy and fulfillment that had once fueled my calling as a teacher were now overshadowed by a sense of hopelessness, and I grappled with the uncertainty of where to go from this disheartening juncture in my career.

In the midst of the darkness, a devastating call shattered my world one late February night. The news of our twenty-seven-year-old nephew's overdose, leading to his untimely death, opened the floodgates in my mind, unleashing a torrent of emotions. The loss of this troubled soul, still a child of God, deeply affected me, bringing back haunting memories of Stetsen's accident from a decade ago. I grappled with conflicting emotions: gratitude that my own son had not suffered the same fate yet burdened with guilt that my nephew's life had been cut short while Stetsen lived on. The tragedy struck me at my core, resurfacing the buried depression and anxieties I had long tried to suppress, all while navigating the challenging circumstances at work. The darkness swiftly enveloped me once more, engulfing me in a profound and quiet intensity.

Following that fateful night, the haunting dreams and nightmares plagued me relentlessly. I found myself immersed in visions of Stetsen's accident, only this time, he didn't survive, and I would be next to join him. Then came the dreams of fleeing through familiar woods, pursued by a relentless unseen presence calling out that there was no escape. Each time I closed my eyes, the nightmares would grip me tightly.

In an attempt to evade the terror, I chose to stop sleeping altogether, enduring two and a half months of sleeplessness and agony. My body couldn't withstand the strain any longer, and I eventually sought help. But before that moment, I felt like giving up on life and everyone in it. My despair became all-consuming, and I stopped leaving my bed, surrendering to the darkness that seemed to have swallowed me whole.

After enduring two and a half months of anguish following our nephew's passing, a breaking point was reached. I was rushed to the hospital from the high school in an ambulance as everyone feared I was having a heart attack. Fortunately, Scott was at the hospital where he worked, and he was there to meet me. It was evident to him that I was in dire straits.

The hospital visit confirmed the severity of the situation: a severe panic attack and a mental breakdown brought on by the physical toll of depression and severe anxiety. I was diagnosed with a severe anxiety disorder and later with post-traumatic stress disorder (PTSD). To quell the panic attacks and help me sleep, doctors prescribed medication, but they also delivered a stern warning: I could not and should not return to the high school, the place that had crushed my spirit.

Yet there was more to the turmoil I was facing than just the situation at the school. It was time to confront the deeper issues no matter how painful the journey to healing might be.

In the following month, my world became a desolate and arduous place. Even with Sierra returning from her mission and requiring surgery for her gallbladder and knee, I found it incredibly difficult to rise from bed. The task felt insurmountable, and I lay there, devoid of thoughts and actions, as if life had drained from my being. My body ached with profound pain, while my mind remained trapped in an impenetrable darkness. Even the sunniest days in Arizona felt bleak and gloomy as the darkness enveloped me entirely, engulfing me in its suffocating grasp. The weight of it all was too overwhelming to bear, making every aspect of life an agonizing struggle.

During those dark days, I distinctly recall Sierra, my daughter, coming in to check on me. She would inquire if I needed anything, though my responses were hardly discernible, if at all. Then one sunny morning, as the brightness of the day contrasted with my inner turmoil, Sierra approached my bedside and sat quietly beside me. Her gentle presence was a stark contrast to the heaviness I felt inside. Unexpectedly, she posed a question that would prove to be a turning point in my thought process. She asked if I had been reading my scriptures and saying my prayers. My initial reaction was to become slightly defensive, wondering why she would ask such a question. However, the sincerity in her eyes and the truth in her words pierced through the darkness as she reminded me that it was a question I would ask her if our roles were reversed. Her words resonated deeply within me, planting a seed of hope and prompting me to reevaluate my spiritual practices as a source of strength and comfort in these trying times.

At first, I felt a surge of anger at Sierra's question. How could she dare ask if I was reading my scriptures and saying my prayers? I believed I had every right to wallow in darkness and despair if I chose to. However, as I reflected on her words, a different perspective emerged. My beautiful recently returned missionary daughter had absorbed something valuable from my teachings, a simple but crucial principle I had instilled in her during her primary years. The reminder to read the scriptures and say prayers had stuck with her, and in that moment, I realized that it was a lesson I needed to revisit as well. Perhaps if I followed these sacred practices, my life could indeed turn around, and I could find solace and strength in trusting the Lord's plan for me. I needed to trust in myself too, to know that I could overcome this trial, that everything I faced was for a reason, a lesson that I needed to learn and eventually pass on to others who would need the same guidance.

I decided to force myself out of that bed and embrace each new day with prayer and Scripture study, resurrecting a lifelong routine that had previously sustained me. Sierra's gentle reminder served as a powerful catalyst, reigniting my commitment to living a purposeful life and offering me hope that my situation could improve.

In the midst of my overwhelming need for help, I found myself grappling with where to turn. Memories of my previous futile search for assistance haunted me, leaving me hesitant and apprehensive about seeking help again. However, I knew deep down that I couldn't endure this struggle on my own any longer. Turning to my husband, Scott, was the first step I took. He had been a witness to my prolonged distress and had repeatedly implored me to allow him to support me. At that moment, I recognized how much I needed him by my side more than I had ever needed anyone before. With trepidation, I finally summoned the courage to ask him to help me find someone I could talk to, someone who was skilled and compassionate enough to provide the assistance I so desperately sought. The fear of rejection, like I had experienced in the past, still haunted me, but I realized that my well-being depended on reaching out and allowing myself to accept the support that was offered.

With unwavering determination, Scott embarked on a mission to find the help I so desperately needed. He reached out to nurses and doctors at the hospital, seeking recommendations for a therapist who could provide the support and guidance I sought. A close friend eventually suggested a therapist, and she wasted no time in meeting with me after hearing my story. From the moment we started our sessions, she proved to be an invaluable lifeline, saving me from the depths of despair.

But the journey to healing was far from easy. Opening up to her was a daunting and challenging task as I had to confront and release the overwhelming weight of guilt and anger I harbored over Stetsen. Nights spent sleepless with worry over his well-being, along with the regrets of how I handled the situation, consumed me. I grappled with the unrelenting burden of "mom shame" that lingers when we make mistakes with our children, struggling to let go of the past even though I knew I needed to. Throughout the therapeutic process, she patiently coaxed me to open doors I had shut tightly, gently prying and delving deeper to help me confront these deeply rooted emotions I had been holding on to for so long.

As I delved into the nightmares with my therapist, she probed deeper, wanting to understand why I was running through the woods, away from someone calling out to me. Inevitably, the memories of being stalked by my colleague years before came pouring out. The floodgates opened, and the nightmare of those dark years unfolded before us. As I recounted the harrowing experiences, we both found ourselves in tears—I sobbing uncontrollably and she silently crying alongside me. It was a powerful moment of raw emotion, a breakthrough that allowed me to finally confront the reality that I had been stalked. With her guidance, I labeled that event for what it truly was, and it was time to face it head-on.

Admitting once again that I had allowed this to happen was agonizingly difficult. However, my therapist showed me that it was not my fault that he had chosen to stalk me, and I needed to recognize that this burden was his to bear, not mine. To break free from being his victim, I had to learn to let go and release myself from the chains of guilt and shame that had kept me captive for so long. It would take several therapy sessions, but I gradually began to see that finding strength within myself and letting go was the key to reclaiming my life and my sense of self.

The journey of forgiveness began, and it was a formidable task. I knew it was time to forgive those who had hurt me, to release the grip of old grudges and judgments that had been weighing me down. It all started with forgiving Stetsen. Despite my attempts to control and the regrets I carried, I had to find it in my heart to forgive him for the pain he caused me.

And then I had to forgive myself for the moments of perceived failure and shortcomings as a mother. It was challenging to let go of the notion of being a perfect parent, realizing that there is no one-size-fits-all manual for raising each unique child entrusted to us. Seeking God's forgiveness for my inadequacies as a mother proved to be the most arduous task of all. It felt overwhelmingly difficult to forgive myself even though I understood it was a commandment. But gradually, through introspection and spiritual reflection, I began to experience the healing power of forgiveness. I learned to accept God's love and forgiveness, allowing it to permeate my life and mend the broken pieces of my soul. It was a long and trying process, but I finally found the strength to forgive myself and embrace the profound love and grace bestowed upon me by a merciful Heavenly Father.

Forgiveness was a formidable but essential step in my healing journey. I knew I needed to forgive the individuals who had caused me so much heartache: the man who stalked me, the toxic principal, the hurtful neighbor, the harsh Relief Society president, and others who had offended me over the years. My therapist encouraged me to write letters to each of them, expressing my feelings and extending forgiveness. Reading those letters aloud was too difficult for me, but just the act of writing them allowed me to release the burden I had been carrying. I felt a weight lifted off my shoulders, and my heart grew lighter.

The transformation was evident in my countenance as the act of forgiveness had a profound impact on my well-being. While people often say, "Forgive and forget," I found it challenging to forget entirely. Instead, I chose to remember the lessons I had learned while letting go of the negative feelings associated with those individuals. Forgiveness allowed me to embrace a sense of freedom and find strength in understanding the reasons forgiveness is crucial for my own growth and healing.

The persistent presence of my former superintendent in my thoughts and dreams puzzled me deeply. His passing the year before seemed to have left unresolved feelings between us. In my dreams, he appeared, seemingly seeking my forgiveness, as if he needed it to find peace on the other side. It felt as though he was trapped in a state of needing my forgiveness to find closure and forgive himself.

But I couldn't grasp the reason for this need. What was it that I needed to forgive him for? Why did he need my forgiveness now when he was no longer in this world? The questions swirled in my mind, and I was compelled to confront this aspect of my healing journey, seeking answers to the unexplained presence of my former superintendent in my thoughts and dreams.

As I shared my perplexing dilemma with Scott, he offered insights into the situation with my former superintendent. While acknowledging his good intentions as an educator, Scott pointed out the complexities of his role in a small town, where certain influential families held significant sway. The community's pressures and expectations likely influenced his decisions and actions. However, Scott reminded me of the critical role my former superintendent played during the time of stalking and how his actions could have possibly prevented the situation from escalating further. Scott suggested that my forgiveness might be the key to allowing him to find peace in the afterlife, that I held the power to release him from any lingering burdens.

These poignant words resonated deeply within me, and I recognized that it was time for me to let go of any lingering resentment and grant him the forgiveness he needed to find closure and move on. It was a difficult but essential step for both him and me on our paths to healing.

In a moment of profound reflection and self-examination, I faced the complexities of my past interactions with my former boss and mentor. I acknowledged the times when I needed his support and understanding yet felt let down and discouraged. However, I also recognized the times when he was there for me, guiding and mentoring me to become a better educator. Through this introspection, I understood the importance of granting him the forgiveness he needed to find peace and move forward in the afterlife, so I humbled myself before my Heavenly Father, offering a heartfelt prayer of forgiveness for those moments of disappointment and rejection. I prayed with sincerity, wishing for him to be released from any lingering burdens or regrets.

The peace that followed these prayers was undeniable, and I knew that my former boss had indeed heard my plea for forgiveness and that he was now able to continue his journey in the afterlife with newfound peace. I had played my part in releasing him from any residual negativity, and in doing so, I also found a sense of peace and closure within myself.

Throughout nearly a year of dedicated therapy, I embarked on a transformative journey to reclaim my voice, which had felt stifled and silenced for far too long. As the healing process unfolded, I experienced a profound strengthening of my relationships with both my husband and my children. A newfound connection blossomed, bridging the gaps that had formed over the challenging years. My husband and I worked together to rebuild what had been broken and lost, nurturing a love that now flourished with newfound understanding and support. The shadows of depression and anxiety began to recede, allowing the light of happiness and contentment to flood back into my life.

Christ and my Heavenly Father embraced me with boundless love and compassion, not only for my achievements but for the resilience I had shown in overcoming adversities. As I rekindled my connection with them, I knew I was on the path to healing and rediscovering the strong, independent woman I once was. I found myself basking in the brightness of a life filled with hope, joy, and a renewed sense of purpose.

Rediscovering my passion for teaching was a pivotal moment in my journey of healing and self-discovery. With newfound courage and determination, I sought teaching positions at local community colleges, eager to step back into the familiar environment of a classroom. Despite the challenges I faced during the difficult year of my breakdown, I refused to give up on my dreams. While I chose to step away from administrative roles, I knew deep within me that I would forever be a teacher at heart. Embracing this truth, I reconnected with my purpose, drawing strength from the fulfillment that teaching brought to my life. As I stood before my students once again, I knew that I had reclaimed an essential part of myself, and I was ready to make a difference in their lives, just as they had done for me.

The night of darkness that occurred over fifteen years ago remains etched in my memory as a constant reminder of my resilience and the need to overcome challenges. It serves as a beacon to guide me through the darkest times when I feel lost and unable to see the light. I have learned to embrace the struggle and fight my way out of the darkness, knowing that there is a purpose behind everything that happens in life. With the motto "everything happens for a reason" as my guiding principle, I press forward, knowing that each trial I endure will ultimately lead to growth and strength. I hold on to the belief that as I navigate this life, with its ups and downs, God and Christ will be there to welcome me with open arms when I return home, able to say, "Well done, my good and faithful daughter."

I aspire to leave behind a legacy that resonates with my posterity, one that emphasizes the significance of trials and their role in personal growth and progression. I hope they understand the value of seeking help when needed, recognizing that it is okay to share burdens and find support through professional assistance. My legacy should stand as an embodiment of forgiveness, showing them how to release old hurts and burdens while retaining the lessons learned.

I want to instill in them empathy for others facing similar struggles so they can be a compassionate and understanding presence for those in need, especially during times of deep depression and severe anxiety. Ultimately, I hope my legacy is one of a sympathetic ear and an empathic soul, always ready to help and serve with a heart full of forgiveness.

This journey through life's trials and challenges has been a testament to the strength of the human spirit and the power of forgiveness and healing. It has highlighted the importance of seeking help when needed and the impact of empathy and understanding in supporting others on their own paths. Through the darkest moments, there is hope, and by facing our fears and confronting our pain, we can emerge stronger and more resilient.

My hope is that this story serves as a reminder that we are not alone in our struggles and that it is never too late to find healing, reconnect with our passions, and leave a legacy of love, forgiveness, and compassion for future generations. May we all strive to embrace the lessons learned and continue to grow in faith, grace, and the pursuit of a fulfilling life.

> Often we do not know what we can endure
> until after a trial of our faith.
> —Robert D. Hales

Chapter 8

SERVING THOSE AROUND ME

And behold, I tell you these things that you may learn wisdom;
That you may learn that when ye are in the
Service of your fellow beings;
You are only in the service of your God.

—Mosiah 2:17

Stepping off the activity bus after a grueling cheer practice one late October afternoon at the age of fifteen, the sound of my growling stomach echoed in my ears, a constant reminder of my insatiable hunger. That particular day had been etched into my memory due to the relentless demands it placed on me as a typical high school teenager: juggling schoolwork, tests, and cheerleading practice—all while trying to find time to chat with friends. It started with a rushed morning, running late for seminary at 6:00 a.m. and realizing I had forgotten my lunch, leaving me with an unsatisfying school meal.

Throughout the day, I struggled to keep my energy up, barely eating enough to sustain myself. However, there was a glimmer of comfort in the anticipation of returning home. Knowing my mom's culinary skills, I could almost taste the aroma of a delightful, mouth-watering dinner that awaited me. As I walked up the lane to our home, I was certain that my hunger would soon be appeased, and the weariness of the day would dissipate, replaced by the warmth and nourishment of a lovingly prepared family meal.

As I stepped through the door, a bustling scene greeted me: my mom, adorned in her apron, gracefully orchestrating the kitchen with pots and pans, while my eager brothers and sisters eagerly waited for dinner to be served. The tantalizing aroma emanating from the kitchen filled the air, promising a delightful feast ahead. However, my attention was diverted when I noticed my mom hurriedly wrapping up the dinner preparations. She grabbed pans and tin foil, all while engaged in a phone conversation. She assured the person on the other end that there was plenty of food, promising to be there in fifteen minutes.

Curiosity piqued, I watched as she loaded the car with the scrumptious meal, the delightful scent trailing after her, now absent from the kitchen and our home. As she called back to me, her voice filled with warmth, she asked me to take over and make pancakes for my siblings, explaining that she would return shortly. Pancakes—the reliable go-to when our family's generosity extended to feeding others in need. It was then that I realized, once again, the true essence of family: not only sharing a delicious meal together but also extending that love and care to others within our community, making our home a place of nourishment, not just for ourselves but for those seeking warmth and comfort too.

In my household, this was a regular occurrence: my mom selflessly cooking meals for families in need, carefully wrapping them up to be delivered with compassion. Throughout my life, I had witnessed countless instances of her reaching out to others, sharing her blessings abundantly. Despite our family's modest means, my mom never allowed it to hinder her from serving those who required help. Every day, she would teach us through her heartfelt prayers, seeking guidance from God to lead her toward those in need of her service. The Spirit's guidance would always answer her prayers, directing her to those who specifically required her unique brand of care. Never hesitant to fulfill her callings, she was always willing to serve wherever the need arose, never declining the Lord's call to be of assistance. Her exemplary actions left an indelible mark on my life, shaping how I would serve others throughout my own journey, inspired by her selflessness and love for those in need.

In my life, my husband, Scott, stands as a shining example of what it means to be of service. Always the first to step forward and volunteer, he is the person who receives phone calls from those seeking help and readily answers their pleas. I can still hear his voice calling out to me, informing me that he's rushing off to aid someone in need, the sound fading as he hops into the car, eager to assist others. Countless times, he has spent his own time baking chocolate chip cookies to bring a smile to someone's face. His unwavering support extends to family, friends, church members, and neighbors. There's never a shortage of people he's willing to help. The hours he has dedicated to serving others seem immeasurable, and his selflessness serves as an inspiration to everyone around him, including me. Scott's boundless spirit of service is the guiding light that motivates me to embrace the same compassionate and giving nature in my own life.

At the core of my life's principles lies the servant-leadership model, a philosophy that guides my actions and decisions. For me, leadership is not about exerting authority but about embracing the responsibility to serve those I lead. It entails rolling up my sleeves and getting in the trenches, walking alongside those I am privileged to lead. Actively listening to their concerns, displaying empathy, and being attuned to their needs are vital aspects of this approach. I am committed to being present and available when others require my support, and I constantly seek guidance from my loving Heavenly Father, asking how I can best be of service.

This commitment is unwavering as I am prepared to set aside my own priorities to help others, just like my mom and my husband, Scott, have shown me. Whether it's making pancakes for my family or rushing to assist someone in need, I strive to meet people where they are and offer my help without hesitation, exemplifying the essence of true servant leadership in every aspect of my life.

Throughout the majority of my married life, I have been intimately involved with the Young Women's program. At the tender age of twenty-three, I received my first calling as the Young Women's president, a daunting responsibility as Samantha was merely three years old and Stetsen just a year. Incredibly, I found myself a mere five years older than some of the Young Women I was meant to lead. Years later, fate would see me called as the Young Women's president once again, leading me to emotionally approach my bishop with tears in my eyes, questioning what I had not yet grasped from my previous experience. This journey through the Young Women's program has been a profound one, teaching me valuable life lessons, nurturing my own growth, and guiding me to be an empathetic, compassionate leader for these young souls in their formative years.

I was well aware of the tremendous effort required to support and guide those young girls as their president in the Young Women's program. It was a responsibility that weighed heavily on my shoulders, demanding my wholehearted commitment. The Young Women's program wasn't just a casual involvement; it demanded everything I had to offer. Countless hours were devoted to serving and caring for these young minds and souls, dedicating myself to their growth and well-being. My days were filled with prayers, spending hours on my knees, seeking divine guidance to understand what and how to teach them, striving to connect with them on a deeper level. My constant prayer was to remain aware of their unique needs and challenges.

To fulfill this calling effectively, it required not only my heart, mind, and strength, but also an unwavering trust in the Lord's guidance and wisdom. Being the Young Women's president these girls needed was a commitment that demanded all of me, but it was a journey of growth, love, and profound fulfillment as I witnessed the positive impact on their lives and the strong bonds formed within the Young Women's community.

The first time I received my call to the Young Women's program, we were living in a small town in Northern Arizona. At the outset, only two out of the twelve girls were attending church on Sundays, and for our Wednesday night activities, getting even one girl to attend was a rare occurrence, maybe once a month. As a young woman myself, the weight of this responsibility felt immense even though I had supportive leaders by my side.

Determined to make a positive impact, I fervently turned to prayer each night, seeking divine guidance on how to best serve these girls. The inspiration came to me, urging me to conduct visits as a crucial aspect of my role as the Young Women's president, to view my time with them as a rescue mission, a personal mission. My task was clear: I needed to go to each girl's home, establish genuine connections, understand their individual circumstances firsthand, and empathize with their situations. The message was clear: I was to meet them where they were, offering support and guidance in a way that was both relevant and meaningful to each young woman's unique journey.

The profound wisdom shared by Elder Dale G. Renlund regarding the development of meaningful relationships resonated deeply with me. He emphasized that to truly serve others, we must strive to see them through Heavenly Father's eyes, recognizing the intrinsic value of each soul. It is only when we grasp the immense worth of every individual that we can begin to fathom the boundless love our Heavenly Father has for each of His children.

As I embarked on my rescue mission in the Young Women's program, these words struck a chord with me, for they mirrored the guidance I received from the Holy Ghost. Taking this powerful advice to heart, I committed myself to approach every young woman with a genuine understanding of their unique worth and potential, seeking to serve and uplift them in a way that honored their individuality and divine nature. With this perspective, my service became more purposeful, and the connections I fostered with these young souls grew deeper, driven by the same love and compassion that our Heavenly Father has for all His children.

During this pivotal time, my husband, Scott, was fully immersed in the Young Men's program as the scoutmaster while also working as a dedicated police officer in our town. With the weight of my rescue mission in the Young Women's program, I recognized the necessity of assistance in caring for my young children Samantha and Stetsen while fulfilling my calling. Seeking guidance and support, I confided in my bishop, who proved to be a source of inspiration and understanding, intimately familiar with the needs of our ward members.

Recognizing the importance of my mission and my responsibilities as a mother, he promptly arranged for a babysitter, an older sister from our ward who grew to cherish my two children as her own. This angelic presence proved to be a blessing beyond measure, always there to lend a helping hand whenever needed, enabling me to wholeheartedly dedicate myself to my rescue mission in the Young Women's program. With this remarkable support system in place, I was able to carry out my calling with renewed purpose, knowing that my children were in loving and capable hands.

Moreover, I came to truly understand the significance of Girls' Camp during my time as a leader. As a young woman, I had always cherished the experience of attending Girls' Camp, but being on the other side as a leader held even greater power. Girls' Camp offered a unique opportunity to bring the girls to a serene, picturesque location surrounded by God's breathtaking beauty. It was during this time that the girls let their guards down, allowing me to form strong connections with them as we spent twenty-four hours a day together for five days. These moments at Girls' Camp were when meaningful conversations took place, and I learned about each girl in a way only this setting could provide. The impact of Girls' Camp on their testimonies was profound, leaving a lasting impression throughout their lives. The valuable lessons they learned during those days would be carried forward, shaping their futures and guiding their choices. For me, Girls' Camp was where my rescue efforts found fulfillment as I witnessed the transformative power it had on these young souls, fostering growth, unity, and a deepening of their connection with God.

Our time in this small town spanned merely three years, but within that short period, Scott and I experienced and achieved an extraordinary amount. As we departed, we left behind a transformed Young Women's program—all twelve young women were consistently attending both Sunday and Wednesday meetings. The last year's Girls' Camp was a testament to the program's impact, with nearly all of them in attendance, basking in the Spirit, who had become an integral part of their lives. The poignant tears shed during the final fast-and-testimony meeting before our departure were a reflection of the profound connection these young women had formed with the program, demonstrating the strength and depth of the Spirit's influence. These girls had undoubtedly changed my life for the better, and witnessing their radiant faces at church was the ultimate reward, a testament to the power of service and the profound difference it can make in the lives of others.

The second time I received the call to serve as the Young Women's president, I found myself in a ward where the girls struggled with unkindness and division. Cliques had formed within the various classes, and the atmosphere on Sundays and Wednesdays was rife with contention. Overcoming this immense challenge became my primary mission: to establish a unified program built on kindness and the influence of Christ in their lives. It was a daunting task, one that made me feel unworthy and inadequate, but I clung to the belief that the Lord qualifies those He calls.

With unwavering faith in His guidance and grace, I embarked on this journey, determined to create an environment where these young women could experience the true spirit of unity, love, and understanding. My goal was to help them see Christ's example and teachings in action, nurturing their relationships with one another and fostering an atmosphere of compassion and acceptance. Through His guidance and the collective effort of dedicated leaders and girls, we gradually began to witness a transformation within the Young Women's program as love and harmony prevailed over discord, and the spirit of kindness infused our meetings, paving the way for growth, friendship, and a stronger connection with the divine.

The initial month of my second stint as Young Women's president was an absolute nightmare. Each time we gathered, be it Sundays or Wednesdays, I would leave the building in tears. The atmosphere was riddled with meanness among the girls, directed not only toward one another but also toward me. It seemed like an insurmountable challenge, exacerbated by the discontent of some parents who were unhappy with my appointment. We were relatively new to the ward, and many were skeptical about my ability to lead effectively. Even I had doubts about my capabilities, questioning if I was up to the task. Despite my fervent prayers, I struggled to see a clear path forward. The issues faced by the girls felt overwhelming, and I wondered if I could handle them even with the Lord's help. Doubts clouded my mind, and I felt lost, unsure of where to even begin. The obstacles ahead seemed insurmountable, and I yearned for clear guidance from above.

One particular Sunday, I returned home in tears, deeply hurt by the unkindness displayed by two of the girls. Throughout the lesson, they would loudly challenge the truths I presented while also exhibiting cruelty toward their peers in the class. These girls believed they had the right to do as they pleased, fueled by their popularity, beauty, and athleticism, making them intimidating figures akin to "mean girls."

To add to my distress, one of the girl's mothers confronted me in the hallway, expressing that her daughter no longer wished to attend Young Women's because I failed to make it enjoyable for her and singled her out. Moreover, she criticized my lack of productivity in our Wednesday activities. It felt as though I had been thrust into an intense, relentless fire, and no one was there to rescue me. The weight of the situation was crushing, and I struggled to see a way out of this challenging and emotionally draining circumstance.

Amidst the turmoil and challenges, Scott sat me down and posed a pivotal question: did I want to be released from my calling or continue despite the difficulties? It would have been the easier path to request a release, believing it would alleviate the strain. However, I couldn't bring myself to take the easy way out. Instead, I turned to prayer with unparalleled intensity, pouring my heart out to the Lord. I trusted that if I listened intently, an answer would come. And it did. A radiant light filled my heart and soul, illuminating an idea that took root within me, a plan that I knew was divinely directed by my Heavenly Father. This inspired plan became my guiding beacon through the challenges ahead, providing me with the strength and clarity I needed to face the obstacles head-on. My unwavering faith and commitment to seeking divine guidance showed me that with His help, I could find a path through the darkness, instilling hope and determination within me to persevere and make a positive difference in the lives of these young women.

The plan that unfolded before me, which I aptly named the "Good Works Unification Plan," centered on cultivating awareness and appreciation for the acts of service occurring around us. I envisioned a way to help the girls recognize the kindness and support extended to them by others, making them more aware of the people who cared about their well-being and understood their individual needs.

The plan was elegantly straightforward. I distributed small square pieces of paper as tools to implement this vision. On these pieces of paper, the girls were encouraged to jot down any instances of kindness, service, or support they experienced from family, friends, or community members. This exercise allowed them to acknowledge and value the good deeds that often go unnoticed in the rhythms of daily life. Through the Good Works Unification Plan, the girls would come to appreciate the interconnectedness of their lives with those around them, fostering a culture of gratitude, empathy, and unity within the Young Women's program and beyond. It was a small yet powerful step toward creating a community of love and appreciation, led by the inspiration I believed was divinely directed.

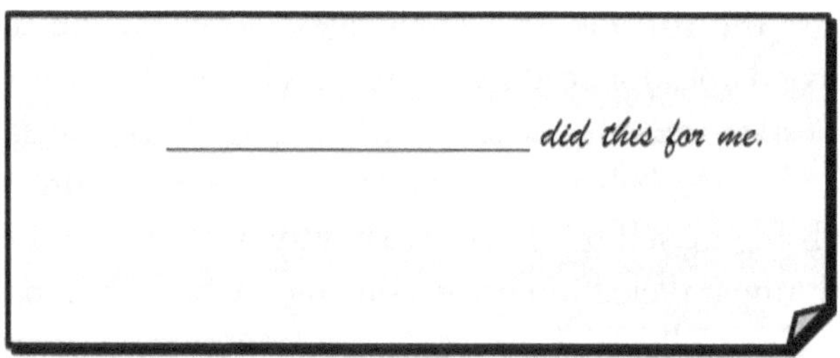

Inspired by the Good Works Unification Plan, the girls eagerly engaged in recording the acts of service performed for them, noting the names of those who had brightened their days. To visualize their collective efforts, I created a chart with a thermometer design, complete with lines marking the increments, except this thermometer measured the number of good deeds rather than degrees. The girls were encouraged to fill the thermometer with the count of good works they received from others, nurturing a sense of appreciation and gratitude for the kindness bestowed upon them. The catch was that they couldn't list the good deeds they had done for others, only those done for them.

To incentivize their participation, I shared that if we collectively filled the thermometer with good works, we would embark on a special trip to the Mesa, Arizona, temple in April to attend the Easter Pageant. The excitement grew as we planned an overnight journey to Mesa, staying with a welcoming family member, enjoying dinner together, and witnessing the powerful Easter Pageant on Friday night. The weekend would conclude with a leisurely day of shopping on Saturday, making this trip a memorable and rewarding celebration of the goodness and kindness the girls had experienced within their community.

The girls initially embraced the idea of the trip but were uncertain about the good-works aspect. However, it didn't take long for them to catch on and wholeheartedly embrace the concept. With only four months until the pageant, their desire to embark on the journey motivated them to engage in the Good Works Unification Plan wholeheartedly.

As the program gained momentum, the service rendered among the girls was truly heartwarming and inspiring. They reported instances where a girl felt lonely during lunch, and another young woman reached out to keep her company, erasing her solitude. In another touching example, a girl having a tough day was surprised with cookies anonymously left at her doorstep, bringing tears of gratitude and comfort. The transformation was evident: their hearts were changing, and their countenances radiated positivity. The girls became more cohesive, getting along harmoniously and actively participating in Sunday lessons and Wednesday activities. The sense of unity and love among them as young women in the gospel blossomed, and the Spirit was felt powerfully throughout their interactions. The Good Works Unification Plan had sparked a beautiful change, fostering an environment of love, kindness, and compassion among the young women, leaving an indelible mark on their lives and the Young Women's program.

The Good Works Unification Plan proved to be a resounding success, leading to a memorable trip to the Easter Pageant, an experience the girls cherished and reminisced about for years to come. The transformation was evident during Girls' Camp that year. The girls started to view each other in a new light as the light of Christ shone brightly within them. Through acts of service, they cultivated a deeper appreciation for one another and began to blossom into beautiful young women, both inwardly and outwardly.

My love for these spirited young women grew immensely as the years passed, witnessing not only the strong bonds they formed with each other but also the growth in their faith and relationship with their Heavenly Father. The radiance of Christ's light in their countenances was a testament to the profound impact of their collective efforts and the power of love and service. The reward I sought was found in the profound transformation of these young souls, their unity, and their strengthened connection with God.

The subsequent years of serving as their Young Women's president were adorned with cherished and fond memories. The spirit of good works lived on beyond the thermometer and the slips of paper. It had become ingrained in the very fabric of these young women's lives. They embraced the essence of service, not just as a planned activity but as a natural way of living. The transformation was evident: they eagerly served one another, finding joy and blessings that could only be experienced through acts of kindness and selflessness. The unity and love among them flourished, and the Young Women's program became a nurturing environment where service and compassion were the guiding principles. As their Young Women's president, witnessing the profound impact of this change on their lives was a heartwarming and rewarding experience, solidifying my love and admiration for these remarkable young women who had grown into strong and caring disciples of Christ.

The transformation of the two girls who had initially posed the greatest challenges was nothing short of remarkable. As they opened their hearts to serving others, they began to see the light of Christ radiating in those around them. The profound impact of service became evident in their lives as they received and recognized the blessings that flowed from their selfless actions. These two young women, who were once a source of difficulty, grew to become some of my most cherished and beloved individuals. My love for them deepened with each passing day.

In the years that followed, I joyfully received their wedding announcements and birth announcements, and we connected as friends on social media. They taught me invaluable lessons, most notably the power of seeing others as Christ sees them and helping them cultivate the same compassionate perspective. Witnessing their growth and transformation brought me immense joy, and I treasured the privilege of being part of their journey toward becoming Christlike disciples.

Over the span of more than two decades, countless young women crossed paths with me, as I wholeheartedly served in the Young Women's program, a program truly inspired and capable of changing lives. It became my life's mission, and throughout those twenty years, I was blessed to share this journey with my three beloved daughters. We forged treasured memories together in a youth program that held a special place in my heart.

Over nineteen years, I found myself returning to Girls' Camp, attending alongside my beautiful daughters, first as a Young Women's president then as a ward leader, and eventually as a Stake Young Women's leader. These years were filled with dedication to serving the youth, imparting to them the knowledge of their immense potential both in the gospel and in life. The memories of countless lives transformed through the love of Christ are etched deeply in my heart, a testament to the profound impact of serving in this inspired program. It has been a privilege and an honor to guide, uplift, and inspire these remarkable young women as they grow and flourish in their journey of discipleship.

The principles of servant leadership that I had embraced during my time as a district and school administrator remained steadfast. Throughout my various administrative projects and roles, I made it a priority to stand beside the teachers, never forgetting the experiences and challenges they faced in the classroom. My mission was to find meaningful ways to minister to them, to transcend the traditional administrator role and serve in the trenches alongside them. Side by side, I sought to uplift and empower teachers, fostering a genuine connection with not only them but also with fellow administrators. Embracing the notion that it takes a village to raise a child, I kept the students' and children's well-being at the forefront, which allowed me to approach my colleagues, teachers, and fellow administrators as partners in our shared work. My purpose was to make their lives easier, more productive, and fulfilling.

As a servant leader, I deeply cared for and advocated for them, striving to make decisions that were in the best interest of both the teachers and the students. This approach brought immense joy, as my passion for education extended not only to the students but also to the teachers. Together, we worked to create a thriving educational community where everyone felt safe, protected, and well cared for, ensuring a nurturing environment for learning and growth within our district and schools.

The profound joy of ministering with all one's heart, might, mind, and strength cannot be overstated. This lesson was etched deeply into my heart during my pregnancy with my son Stetsen. Conceiving and carrying children had always been a challenge for me; my body was not naturally predisposed to having many babies. Throughout my pregnancy, I endured relentless illness and struggled to gain and maintain weight. My uterus presented complications that threatened to lead to preterm labor, an ordeal I faced in each of my pregnancies.

Despite these daunting challenges, I learned the true essence of ministering: the selfless act of giving our best efforts to care for and uplift others. During those trying times, I experienced the love and support of others who ministered to me, witnessing firsthand the transformative power of genuine care and concern. This experience imbued in me a deep sense of gratitude and a desire to reciprocate, to minister to others with the same love and compassion that had been shown to me. Ministering became a profound and transformative part of my life, shaping my understanding of true discipleship and reinforcing the importance of extending kindness and support to those in need.

Stetsen's pregnancy proved to be one of the most challenging times of my life. Right from the beginning, I was plagued by debilitating illness, making it difficult to keep anything down. Throughout the entire pregnancy, I experienced persistent bleeding, leading to frequent bouts of dehydration. The situation took a dangerous turn when, at twenty-eight weeks, I unexpectedly went into labor, and Scott rushed me to the doctor. By the time they managed to halt the labor, I had already dilated to a four. The doctor prescribed bed rest and medication to prevent further complications, but the side effects of the medication only exacerbated my sickness. For the next eleven weeks, I found myself confined to bed as my two-and-a-half-year-old daughter Samantha frolicked around me, watching *The Little Mermaid* on repeat. To this day, the sight of that movie triggers memories of those difficult and exhausting days of bed rest.

During those challenging eleven weeks of bed rest, my heart was touched by the kindness of my dear visiting teacher, as we were called back then. She was an extraordinary woman, older and single, with a demanding job and the responsibility of caring for her elderly parents in our ward. Despite her already-busy schedule and numerous commitments, this compassionate sister selflessly brought me meals three times a week. I was deeply moved by her genuine concern and generosity. Her consistent support was a lifeline during that difficult time, easing the burden on me and my family. Knowing that we would be taken care of meant one less worry on my mind. With the meals she provided, we had more than enough to last at least two days each time, allowing me the comfort of not needing to get up each day to prepare a meal. Beyond the tangible assistance, her visits became a cherished opportunity for me to have adult conversation and spend precious time with someone outside the confines of my bed rest. I will forever be grateful for the love and care she showed me during those weeks, a beautiful example of Christlike service that left a lasting impact on my heart.

The precious sister who lovingly cared for me during those eleven weeks of bed rest taught me the profound essence of ministering. She exemplified that true service lies not in grand gestures but in the simplicity of being there for others in their time of need. She met me where I was, taking the time to help and support me one meal at a time, making those challenging weeks bearable and livable. Through her selfless actions, she showed me that serving others is not a sacrifice but a privilege and a blessing. Her loving service and genuine care made a lasting impact on my understanding of ministering.

Sadly, a few years later, she passed away from cancer when Stetsen was just seven years old. Her passing served as a poignant reminder of the fleeting nature of life, and I strive to honor her memory by embracing the true spirit of ministering: to render service with my whole heart, viewing it not as a duty but as a gift of love. I am deeply grateful for the lessons she taught me and endeavor each day to follow in her footsteps, ministering as she would have done: with compassion, empathy, and a heart full of love.

In her powerful address during the April 2018 general conference, Sis. Jean B. Bingham conveyed the significance of our service to others as a reflection of our discipleship and our love for God and Jesus Christ.[3] As mortal beings, our purpose on this earth is to strive to become more Christlike and to return to our Heavenly Father with honor. In this journey of discipleship, ministering becomes a crucial aspect, providing us with ample opportunities to emulate our Savior's compassion and selflessness.

Pres. Spencer W. Kimball, in his October 1980 general conference address, wisely urged us to always be mindful of the members of our flock who may be sad, lonely, bereaved, or in distress, for there are always individuals in need of our special care and attention.[4] It is vital to be aware of those around us and to be willing to extend a helping hand, whether it be through providing meals, offering companionship to the lonely, or simply being there to listen and support. The Spirit will guide us to recognize those in need of our unique service, enabling us to make a meaningful difference in their lives. Through ministering with genuine love and compassion, we align ourselves with the Savior's example and fulfill our divine mission of spreading His light and love to all those we encounter.

The essence of service extends beyond acts of kindness to include the profound gift of lifelong friendships. In my journey through this

---

[3] . Jean B. Bingham, "Ministering as the Savior Does," *Ensign*, May 2018.

[4] . Spencer W. Kimball, "Ministering to the Needs of Members," *Ensign*, November 1980.

life, I have been blessed with two extraordinary friends who have walked alongside me through every twist and turn. These remarkable women are more than just friends; they have become my sisters, connected by the unbreakable bonds within my heart. Regardless of what life throws my way, I can always count on these three sisters to be there for me. They catch me when I stumble, help me navigate life's rough waters, and offer invaluable guidance. Together, we have shared the joy of wedding preparations, the art of mending clothes, and the joys and challenges of raising children. Most importantly, they have been the unwavering pillars I can lean on and confide in, providing a shoulder to cry on during life's toughest moments. Reflecting on my journey, I am humbled by the profound impact these three special sisters have had on shaping who I am today. Kim Marble and Debi Farr are more than friends; they are my sisters now and forever, a testament to the extraordinary power of genuine and enduring friendships.

The legacy I aspire to leave behind is one of being a service-oriented individual and a servant leader. Throughout my life, I hope to be remembered by the teachers I have led as someone who always sought to make their journey easier, leading them with love and service in mind. My greatest desire is for my posterity to see my example and be inspired to become service-oriented individuals themselves. I want them to always be on the lookout for those who are hungry, poor in spirit, sad, hurt, or lonely, extending a helping hand and ministering with their whole heart. I hope that empathy will guide their actions, allowing them to see beyond judgment and to reach out to those in need. Above all, I pray that they will never forget to count their blessings that flow from heaven through every act of service they render, perpetuating a legacy of love and care for others that will bless countless lives for generations to come.

The journey of service, compassion, and leadership has been a profound and transformative one. From my early experiences as a young woman and a mother to my roles as a district and school administrator, the significance of ministering to others with a full heart and selfless love has shaped my life's purpose. Inspired by the examples of those who walked alongside me, I have come to understand that true service lies in the simplest acts of kindness and genuine care for those in need. It is through the legacy of service and the power of lifelong friendships that I hope to pass on the torch of love and compassion to my posterity. May they embrace the calling to be service-oriented individuals, seeking out those who require a helping hand, and ministering with empathy and understanding.

Let us all count our blessings that flow from the service we render as we continue to spread light and love in this world, making it a better place for generations to come. May we all remember the words of Elder Dale G. Renlund:

> To effectively serve others we must see them…through Heavenly Father's eyes. Only then can we comprehend the true worth of a soul and sense the love that Heavenly Father has for all His children.[5]

Let us continue to view one another through the lens of love and compassion, fulfilling our divine purpose in service to one another and bringing joy and comfort to every life we touch.

> As we lose ourselves in the service of others, we discover our own lives and our own happiness.
> —Dieter F. Uchtdorf

---

[5] Dale G. Renlund, "Through God's Eyes," *Ensign*, November 2015.

Chapter 9

MY TESTIMONY OF CHRIST

It is essential for you to have your own testimony in these difficult times, for the testimonies of others will carry you only so far.
—Thomas S. Monson

The memory of my first time standing up in sacrament meeting to bear my testimony remains vivid in my mind even to this day. As a young child, I gazed out at the sea of faces in the chapel, all eyes fixed on me as I began to share my simple yet heartfelt testimony. With sincerity, I expressed my belief in the truthfulness of the church, offering gratitude for my loving parents and siblings. I could see my parents beaming with pride as they watched me speak. Nervously, I hoped that my voice wouldn't betray my anxiety, but the overwhelming sense of faith and conviction within me surpassed any unease. That was the beginning, a seed planted in my heart that would grow day after day. It required nurturing, and I found that nourishment by keeping the commandments and embracing the name of Christ willingly. This commitment remains steadfast as I continue to partake of the sacrament every Sunday, a sacred act that perpetuates the growth of my testimony.

The echoes of my family's testimonies resonate deeply within me. Throughout the years, I've listened to my mom and dad share their unwavering faith in Christ countless times. Even at my dad's funeral, his testimony shone through the cherished memories recounted by friends, siblings, and my mom. The love he had for Christ and his eternal companion, my mom, was evident in every story shared. I witnessed my brother-in-law's testimony carried forward through his children's heartfelt recollections upon his passing: the love he had for his family and his abiding faith that they would be reunited in heaven together forever. These powerful testimonies are a testament to the truth the gospel brings into our lives. To sustain and strengthen these testimonies, we must dedicate ourselves each day to the gospel's principles, living it fully and serving others as Christ did. Through such commitment, we can draw closer to our Savior and find enduring peace and joy in our journey of discipleship.

Pres. Gordon B. Hinckley's words from the April 1998 general conference profoundly resonate with the essence of personal testimony within the context of the church. A testimony holds a sacred and influential place in our lives, capable of transforming our very being. It is not a mere sentiment or expression of gratitude; rather, it is a powerful force that sustains us as we navigate life's journey with unwavering faith right until our last days. To possess a genuine testimony, action is required; it demands our commitment and diligent efforts in living the gospel principles. Becoming a true disciple of Christ necessitates dedicating every fiber of our spiritual soul to His teachings. A genuine testimony becomes evident in our actions, service, and the way we conduct ourselves in our homes. It radiates through the love and respect we show our spouse, the care and guidance we provide to our children and grandchildren, and the overall atmosphere of peace that only a Christ-centered home can exude. A testimony is not just something we speak of; it is something that emanates from the core of our being and permeates every aspect of our lives, leaving a lasting and positive impact on those around us.

Developing a strong testimony requires dedicated effort and consistent nourishment of our soul through fundamental principles instilled in us since our early years. The simple yet powerful concepts of prayer, daily Scripture study, regular attendance at church, and immersing ourselves in the teachings of the gospel play a crucial role in strengthening our faith. Additionally, it calls for an unwavering trust in the Lord and His divine plan for each of us. We must wholeheartedly believe in His wisdom and guidance, acknowledging that the path we tread upon is precisely the one He has designed for us. This path may entail trials and challenges, but with trust in Him, we can overcome them. Trusting in the Lord's love and direction is a constant, lifelong endeavor that empowers us to navigate through life's uncertainties with assurance and peace.

As a part of my lasting legacy, I have chosen to leave my testimony here, not only for my immediate family but also for the future generations of our lineage whom I may never have the chance to meet in this mortal life. I want them to understand the depth of my belief in Christ and the profound significance of His gospel in my life. In my earlier days, I perceived being a member of the Church of Jesus Christ of Latter-day Saints as a set of Sunday activities: reading scriptures, praying at meals, and having family prayer. However, as my spiritual journey unfolded, I came to realize that being a member of the church was an integral part of my identity. It became an intrinsic aspect of who I am and who I aspire to become: a person dedicated to continuous growth, learning, righteousness, and unwavering faith. When I bear my testimony, it is a genuine expression of my convictions, leaving no room for doubt that my beliefs are rooted in truth. Being a member of the church is not just something I do; it is an essential part of my being, shaping my character and guiding my life's purpose. Through sharing my testimony, I hope to instill in future generations the certainty of my beliefs and inspire them to embrace their own faith, anchoring themselves firmly in the gospel of Jesus Christ.

The following is my testimony that I hope will be passed on as a big part of my legacy:

> I bear a fervent testimony that the Church of Jesus Christ of Latter-day Saints is the only true and living church upon the earth today. I am confident that God, my Heavenly Father, loves me unconditionally and personally. My unwavering belief is that Jesus is the living Christ, the divine and immortal Son of God, who is my Redeemer, Savior, the beacon of light, life, and

hope for the entire world. I firmly know that He suffered and was resurrected, atoning for my sins and offering the gift of eternal life. When my journey leads me back to God's kingdom, I am certain that Christ will be there to welcome me home with open arms.

I wholeheartedly embrace Joseph Smith as a true prophet of God, who, as a humble fourteen-year-old boy, experienced the divine manifestation that marked the beginning of the restoration. I have no doubt that the Book of Mormon is a genuine testament of Jesus Christ, translated by the hand of God through Joseph Smith. I offer my unwavering support and sustenance to my church leaders, both local and general, as I am certain that they have been called of God and are inspired to lead and guide us in these challenging times. I firmly believe that the prophet today leads us through divine revelation, helping us navigate through the complexities of our era with God's guidance. My testimony of these truths is resolute, and they form the bedrock of my faith, enriching my life with profound meaning and purpose.

With unwavering conviction, I testify that my prayers are answered, and the responses guide me forward along the divine path set forth by the Lord. I firmly believe that God's hand is present in all aspects of our existence, from the intricate details of our lives to the grandeur of the world around us. His constant presence sustains and supports me as I navigate the challenges of this mortal journey.

I have deep faith in the power of the priesthood, recognizing it as the authority to act in God's name on this earth. This sacred power brings heavenly healing and comfort, manifesting the reality of divine influence in our lives.

Above all, I have an unshakable knowledge that the eternal bonds forged within the temple will keep my family united throughout the eternities. As I strive to remain faithful to the covenants made, I am confident that the blessings promised will be bestowed upon me in this life and beyond.

My love for Christ and our Heavenly Father resonates in every aspect of my being, and I am proud to declare my membership in the Church of Jesus Christ of Latter-day Saints. I state these words and close in the name of Jesus Christ. Amen.

I am filled with a deep sense of gratitude for the journey we have embarked on in this section about testimonies. Reflecting on the significance of personal testimony and the power of faith has reaffirmed my belief in the truths of the gospel. It reminds me of the vital role that prayer, Scripture study, and trust in the Lord play in strengthening our testimonies and guiding us along the path of discipleship. I am reminded of the immense love our Heavenly Father has for each of us and the eternal blessings that await us as we remain steadfast in our covenants.

This chat has inspired me to continue striving to be a true disciple of Christ, living His teachings through love and service. With a renewed commitment to the gospel and a profound sense of purpose, I will cherish the knowledge gained here and carry it with me as I continue my journey in the Church of Jesus Christ of Latter-day Saints. Thank you for this meaningful conversation that has deepened my understanding and strengthened my testimony.

We should remember that bearing a heartfelt testimony is only a beginning. We need to bear testimony, we need to mean it, and most importantly, we need to consistently live it. We need to both declare and live our testimonies.

—Elder David R. Bednar

What Is Your Legacy?

> When our hearts turn to our ancestors, something changes
> inside us. We feel part of something greater than ourselves.
> —Pres. Russell M. Nelson

We find ourselves in truly perilous times, witnessing events that seem to echo the prophecies of the second coming. The COVID-19 pandemic has affected countless lives, and we mourn the loss of those around us. Amidst the turmoil, we see wars, civil unrest, and political divisions—things we never anticipated witnessing in our lifetime. These are unprecedented times, as forewarned in scriptures such as 2 Timothy 3:1, which speaks of the arrival of perilous days.

However, we find solace in the knowledge that the Lord is aware of our struggles and watches over us. Through modern-day prophets, He foretold of the calamities that would befall the earth. As Elder Ronald A. Rasband wisely counseled, even in these trying times, we need not fear if we remain steadfast on the covenant path. By seeking refuge in our spirituality and maintaining our commitment to the gospel, we can find strength, protection, and hope to navigate these challenging times.

These are undoubtedly times of remarkable growth and progress within the church. We witness a surge in people's dedication and commitment to the gospel as the work hastens just as our prophets have foretold. Family history endeavors have gained momentum, connecting families in ways never seen before in our history. The rise in temple work is also notable, with an impressive 168 temples now gracing the earth, many of which I have personally witnessed being built in my lifetime. These positive developments are truly uplifting and bring great joy to the hearts of faithful members.

However, amidst these encouraging signs, we must heed the urgent call from President Russell M. Nelson, who wisely stated during the April 2019 general conference that "time is running out." As we marvel at the growth and blessings within the church, we must also remain vigilant in our efforts to follow the Lord's counsel and prepare ourselves and others for the events that lie ahead. The time for diligent discipleship and spreading the light of the gospel is now, for we live in a momentous era of both great opportunity and great responsibility.

Take a moment to reflect and ask yourself what imprint you wish to leave behind for future generations. What kind of legacy are you crafting for your posterity? Are you intentionally building a Christ-centered home, where love, compassion, and understanding prevail? Do you strive to treat your spouse and children with the same grace and kindness that Christ would extend? Are you willing to see others through the lens of Christ's unconditional love, looking beyond preconceptions and judgments?

In a world that appears to be crumbling around us, there are numerous questions that warrant contemplation and self-evaluation. It is crucial to assess whether we have done enough and taught our children enough to fortify them against the trials we currently face. Now is the time to fortify our homes with faith, love, and righteousness, preparing ourselves and our loved ones to navigate the challenges that lie ahead. By fostering a Christlike perspective and instilling in our families a strong foundation of truth and resilience, we can leave behind a legacy that will endure through generations, offering hope and guidance in these tumultuous times.

In these unprecedented times, it is crucial to cling tightly to the iron rod, holding fast to the principles and teachings of the gospel. A close friend, who serves as a former bishop and currently as the second counselor in the stake presidency, shared a profound insight that resonates deeply with me. He mentioned that the sifting process has begun. This revelation prompts us to introspect and ask ourselves, will we allow ourselves to be swept away with the negative influences of the world, or will we stand resolute in our commitment to the eternal truths we know are right? As we witness the challenges and complexities of the world, are we willing to boldly stand up for what we believe and become witnesses of Christ?

These perilous times call for unwavering faith, courage, and the willingness to be a shining example of Christ's love and teachings amidst uncertainty. As we navigate through this sifting period, may we find strength in our commitment to the gospel, holding fast to the iron rod and being a beacon of light in the darkness.

My heartfelt hope is that my posterity will glean valuable insights from the lessons I have learned throughout my life. I yearn for them to embrace the journey of becoming faithful disciples of Christ, carrying my legacy as an integral part of their own lives. I pray they will fearlessly pursue their passions and purpose, contributing to the betterment of the world we live in. May they perpetuate the tradition of watching for and reaching out to those who may have strayed, extending a hand of love and compassion to rescue the lost sheep. I envision them as individuals of service, guided by the unwavering strength of the iron rod, navigating life with unwavering faith.

And as we reunite in the eternities, my ultimate desire is that we will all be joyfully welcomed home as good and faithful servants, bound together in the eternal embrace of Christ's love and grace.

Your story is the greatest legacy that you will leave to your friends.
It's the longest-lasting legacy you will leave to your posterity.
—Steve Saint

Dr. Stephanie West is an accomplished educator and leader with a passion for educational excellence and innovation. She holds an EdD in organization leadership with an emphasis on educational leadership from Grand Canyon University, Arizona, which she earned in 2019. Her pursuit of academic excellence started with a BA in elementary education from Arizona State University in 2001.

Dr. West's educational journey continued with a master of education in educational administration in 2013 and a master of education in curriculum and instruction, specializing in reading, in 2006, both from Grand Canyon University. Her dedication to professional growth is evident in her extensive list of certifications, including K–8 Elementary Education, K–12 Principal, Superintendent Endorsement, K–12 Reading Specialist, Structured English Immersion, and Early Childhood Education.

As an assistant adjunct professor at Grand Canyon University and Scottsdale Community College, Dr. West has been instrumental in shaping the next generation of educators through teaching and guidance. Her contributions to the field of education can be seen in her academic publications and professional development presentations.

Beyond the illustrious tapestry of Dr. West's scholarly conquests lies a pinnacle of achievement that surpasses all others: her cherished family. As a stalwart mother to three exceptional daughters and a valiant son who serves in the army, she has woven a legacy of devotion, service, and benevolence. It is with ineffable pride that she also commends her daughter-in-law and three esteemed sons-in-law, virtuous souls who enfold her progeny in a cocoon of ardent love and unwavering devotion.

Each of her offspring emanates an aura of service, kindness, and magnanimity, making them not only resplendent in appearance but also in character. Nestled within the cradle of her heart are the nine precious jewels of her existence: her beloved grandchildren, each one lavished with the tender affection that only Grandma can bestow.

Amidst the intricate mosaic of her life's passages, it is her unwavering partnership with her husband, Scott, that stands as the bedrock of her existence. He is her unwavering support, her soul's confidant, and the embodiment of the profound love that has illuminated her journey.

www.ingramcontent.com/pod-product-compliance
Lightning Source LLC
Chambersburg PA
CBHW021001180726

47993CB00017B/527